NETWORKING MAGIC

This is a wonderful book. Informative and intriguing. *Networking Magic* will change your life.

—**John Gray**, Ph.D., author of *Men Are from Mars, Women Are from Venus*

Read this GREAT book and you'll learn how to make extraordinary contacts that will forever change and improve your life.

—**Mark Victor Hansen**, creator of the *Chicken Soup for the Soul* series

Networking will change your life … and this book will get you started!

—**Harvey Mackay**, author of the #1 *New York Times* bestseller *Swim with the Sharks Without Being Eaten Alive*

An absolute winner! Explains how to get it all by networking. A gem on how to build and maintain relationships! Will enrich your life. Not just the ABCs of networking. *Networking Magic* is the whole alphabet.

—**Herb Cohen**, author of *You Can Negotiate Anything* and *Negotiate This*

Networking Magic is pure magic, it opened my eyes. A great informative book! I learned tons from it! Finally, a great information packed book that says it ALL about networking. Destined to become the networker's bible: breezy, easy to read and information packed—I thought I knew networking until I read this amazing book! Frishman and Lublin know networking. Read Networking Magic and you will too. The new, must-read classic on networking. Don't leave home without it!

—**Jack Canfield**, coauthor *Chicken Soup for the Soul* series and CEO of Chicken Soup for the Soul Enterprises

Networking Magic teaches an important principle: that by connecting with and serving others, you also serve yourself. As the authors put it, "Generosity is the soul of networking."

—**Ken Blanchard,** coauthor of *The One Minute Manager* and *The Leadership Pill*

You have to build relationships to be successful today, and *Networking Magic* will show you how to do just that. My one complaint is that this book was not available when I started my business career!

—**Jim McCann**, CEO, 1-800-FLOWERS.COM

Networking Magic is pure magic! From page one, it reads quickly and clearly teaches you how to improve every aspect of your life.

—**Les Brown**, motivational speaker and author of
Live Your Dreams and *Up Thoughts For Down Times*

Networking Magic transforms the invisible ingredients for success into visible, viable and practical action steps. Nobody does it better than Rick and Jill. They have taught me "unless you are networking you soon will be not working!"

—**Dr. Denis Waitley**, author of *The Seeds of Greatness*

Frishman and Lublin have done it again! In *Networking Magic* they reveal the secrets and insights of successful networkers in a manner that is easy and fun to read.

—**Robin Sharma**, author of *The Monk Who Sold His Ferrari*
and *The Saint, the Surfer and the CEO*

From A to Z, *Networking Magic* includes everything you need to know about networking. It's an indispensable book. I wish I'd had a copy when I started publishing twelve years ago!

—**Gregory J. P. Godek**, author of *1001 Ways to Be Romantic*

Make this book your desk bible on how to make positive connections every time you step out of your office and into the marketplace. Your networking strategy will come alive!

—**Mark LeBlanc**, author of *Growing Your Business!*

Networking Magic's simple tools and amazing insights inspire others to help you. It is the "how-to" on achieving success.

—**Romanus Wolter**, "The Kick Start Guy"

Networking Magic is exactly the right book at the right time for anyone trying to get ahead. Frishman and Lublin clearly demonstrate "It's who you know" when it comes to nearly any type of success. If you follow their first-rate easy to understand practical advice you'll soon know everyone!

—**Steven Schragis**, National Director, Learning Annex

This book brings as much spirit and value to your business acumen as Jill Lublin and Rick Frishman add to your personal network. Do yourself a favor by reading their generous and thoughtful book! A great read about a critical and often ignored discipline in business and in life.

—**Tom Ehrenfeld**, author of The Startup Garden:
How Growing a Business Grows You (www.startupgarden.com)

If you want to build successful relationships with others, this book is for you. This book will help you to discover the dynamics of how to make networking work effectively for YOU. Building relationships and creating lots of shameless fans has helped me to grow my business faster than any other marketing strategy I've tried. This book will show you how to be a master at it!

—**Debbie Allen**, award-winning author of
Confessions of Shameless Self Promoters (www.confessionsofshaeless.com)

Networking is a master skill in business and life. This book will show you how to master the art of networking!

—**Sam Silverstein**, CSP (Certified Speaking Professional)

The inside secrets of two networking pros. In *Networking Magic*, Frishman and Lublin teach you how to build and maintain powerful networks that will get you on top and keep you there.

—**Robert Allen**, coauthor of *The One-Minute Millionaire*

The special tactics covered in this book are absolute gems. Here you'll discover a foolproof system for remembering names and many super networking strategies that outperform any other method. Buy it! You won't be sorry.

—**Marilyn Ross**, author of *Shameless Marketing for Brazen Hussies*
and eleven other books (Marilyn@MarilynRoss.com)

If any two people can create networking magic, it's Rick Frishman and Jill Lublin. Being in the communications field myself, I know artists when I see them. When it comes to expanding your "list" and getting the most out of it, these two are artists.

—**Joel Roberts**, media consultant,
former prime-time talk show host KABC Radio, Los Angeles

There is a lot more to life than just "showing up." Frishman and Lublin's new book will make sure that you know how to show up at the right time and place, and meet the right group of people. If networking is important to you, reading this book and heeding its simple, smart advice is the first step you should take.

—**Stephen Burgay,** Senior Vice-President/Corporate Communications, John Hancock Financial Services

Authors and publishers network freely. We do not compete: Since every book is unique, no one feels threatened. This book shows book people how to help each other even more effectively.

—**Dan Poynter**, author of The Self-Publishing Manual (www.parapublishing.com)

If you're fishing for better contacts and bigger business, Lublin and Frishman will expertly show you how to hook those connections and make the magic happen!

—**Randy Peyser**, bestselling author of *Crappy to Happy: Small Steps to Big Happiness NOW!* (www.authoronestop.com)

If you plan to deal with people—at any level—don't make a move without reading *Networking Magic*. It's full of great information and amazing insights on a subject we all need to master.

—**Mike Fink**, International NLP Trainer, Speaker and Consultant, Founder of Magician Within, Inc.

To succeed today, you must be a great networker and *Networking Magic* will show you the way. It's the best, most comprehensive and practical book on networking.

—**Bill Lauterbach of** FIVE STAR Speakers & Trainers, LLC

Networking Magic gives you everything you need to know about networking, and didn't know to ask. In turbulent, fast changing times, you lose if you aren't a savvy schmoozer. This book is a definite Keeper!

—**Dr. Judith Briles**, author of *The Confidence Factor* (www.Briles.com)

All of marketing, all of business, can be broken down to one thing: creating relationships—or, as I like to put it, making friends. If you haven't figured out how to make friends yet, read *Networking Magic*. It could change your life in a very good way.

—**John Kremer**, author of *1001 Ways to Market Your Books*

Frishman and Lublin have done it—again. *Networking Magic* is like a tsunami of fresh air, chock-full of useful, bone-honest insights into a subject important to us all. Thank you for writing this book!

—**Bill Catlette**, workforce guru and coauthor of *Contented Cows Give Better Milk*

Clear, comprehensive and loaded with fabulous stories, *Networking Magic* is the networker's Bible. People will be talking about and using this remarkable new book for years.

—**James F. Barry Jr.**, CFP, financial advisor, author, and host of PBS's *Jim Barry's Financial Success*

I went from flight attendant to published author, by using the principles from *Networking Magic*! Thanks Rick and Jill!

—**Marsha Marks**, author of *101 Simple Lessons for Life*

A sure-fire networking classic! The fastest way to succeed is ultimately about cultivating (and enjoying) the habit of insisting on someone else's success. And it's the only way to ensure that someone, somewhere will insist on yours. And that's where the magic comes in. Every time.

—**Gail Blanke**, CEO/President of Lifedesigns; author of *In My Wildest Dreams*

Networking is the key to success in all realms of our lives. This book will jump-start you.

—**Suzy Allegra**, author of *How to Be Ageless: Growing Better, Not Just Older!*

I love *Networking Magic*. The authors have raised the bar of networking to an art as they describe an enriching lifestyle rather than a series of tactics.

The book is filled with gems—a "must-read" to achieve greater success through building win-win relationships.

—**Lynn Joseph**, Ph.D., Career Transition Consultant and author of *The Job-Loss Recovery Guide: A Proven Program for Getting Back to Work—Fast!*

Networking Magic is a must read. It contains an enormous variety of networking ideas, served up with anecdotes and stories that show exactly how they work. The book is dynamic, delightful and abundantly full of valuable, usable information.

—**Angie Hollerich**, CEP, CCA, owner, Brass Ring Productions, Ltd.; author of *The Weight and Wealth Factors, Grab the Brass Ring of Financial Security, The Wellness Path,* and *Tips From the Top*

Human beings do networking, or connecting, naturally. *Networking Magic* is a fascinating study of how to do it with elegance, grace, generosity and success. This book will teach you how to do it to improve both your business and your personal life.

—**Catherine Jewell**, speaker and author of *STAR Performance*

Networking Magic has everything you need to know about networking from A to Z. This book will help you attract clients and contacts with ease.

—**Caterina Rando**, M.A., MCC, speaker, trainer, and master coach: author of *Learn to Power Think*

Jill Lublin and Rick Frishman are the greatest! Their generous advice and tremendous resources helped my company get the word out. Thank you both for your Magic!

—**Loral L. Langemeier**, M.A., CPPC, founder/CEO of Live Out Loud & WealthDiva.com

This much-needed book is just the ticket for rejection-proofing your networking experiences.

—**Elayne Savage**, Ph.D., author of *Don't Take It Personally!* and *The Art of Dealing with Rejection*

This is Networking 101 at its best. It should be required reading by every business executive. An enriching, inspirational experience ... it will change your business and personal relationship thinking.

—**Hans Helmuth**, CEO, NewBusinessNetwork.Biz

Finally, a common-sense book with techniques everyone can use.

—**Andrea Frank Henkart**, author of *Cool Communication*

Networking Magic is the magic bullet for business success.

—**Cynthia Kersey**, *Unstoppable*

For over 75 years, Welcome Wagon has been providing a networking opportunity for local businesses and new homeowners. *Networking Magic* is the how-to guide for creating connections in today's hectic world.

—**Greg Hebner**, President, Welcome Wagon

NETWORKING
MAGIC
UPDATED 2ND EDITION

*How to Find
Connections
that Transform
Your Life*

RICK FRISHMAN AND JILL LUBLIN

NEW YORK

NETWORKING MAGIC UPDATED 2ND EDITION
How to Find Connections that Transform Your life

Published in New York, New York, by Morgan James Publishing. Morgan James and The Entrepreneurial Publisher are trademarks of Morgan James, LLC. www.MorganJamesPublishing.com

The Morgan James Speakers Group can bring authors to your live event. For more information or to book an event visit The Morgan James Speakers Group at www.TheMorganJamesSpeakersGroup.com.

BitLit
FOR ALL THE BOOKS YOU OWN

FREE eBook edition for your existing eReader with purchase

———————————————
PRINT NAME ABOVE

For more information, instructions, restrictions, and to register your copy, go to **www.bitlit.ca/readers/register** or use your QR Reader to scan the barcode:

ISBN 978-1-61448-734-0 paperback
ISBN 978-1-61448-735-7 eBook
Library of Congress Control Number:
2013945996

Cover Design by:
Rachel Lopez
www.r2cdesign.com

Interior Design by:
Bonnie Bushman
bonnie@caboodlegraphics.com

In an effort to support local communities, raise awareness and funds, Morgan James Publishing donates a percentage of all book sales for the life of each book to Habitat for Humanity Peninsula and Greater Williamsburg.

Get involved today, visit
www.MorganJamesBuilds.com.

Habitat
for Humanity®
Peninsula and
Greater Williamsburg
Building Partner

To my wife Robbi, with love and thanks.

—**Rick Frishman**

To God, who makes my life and light possible. May
I always spread great messages to make a difference in the
world. I am grateful for all your blessings.

—**Jill Lublin**

TABLE OF CONTENTS

ACKNOWLEDGEMENTS

This book is the direct product of networking. It owes its existence to the generous sharing of others, many of whom were strangers when we began this project. Virtually every word, every idea and suggestion that fills these pages was graciously given to us or reinforced by friends, friends of friends, friends of friends friends and so on. Tracing the linkage of all the connections is as hopeless as tracing your thoughts for the month.

We want to thank the people listed below who have made this book a reality. They gave us an outpouring of networking information and made the experience of writing this book magical. Scores of strangers became our collaborators and our friends. They told us their stories, revealed their secrets and explained how their businesses, interests and lives worked. They called us and spoke at length on their dime. They told their friends and contacts, who called us and did the same. They sent us FedEx packages stuffed with their books, promotional materials, audios, videos and their thoughts. They gave and gave and gave.

People we never met invited us to dinners, to meetings, conferences, into their homes and into their lives. Many took the time to write long, detailed emails and happily answered all of our questions and follow-up calls. After we spoke, they contacted us to ask if we needed additional information and sent us thank-you notes. They continually gave far more than we asked or even expected and were, and still are, willing to give even more. Our friends and collaborators not only gave us information, they shared their secrets and allowed us to publish the fruits of their wisdom in a book we planned to sell.

Speakers and authors of networking books, established and recognized authorities, who could have considered us competitors, willingly provided their help. They showered us with information, stories and quotes. Instead of treating us as rivals, they acted as if we were new kids in the community—the networking community. They welcomed us, mentored us and seemed happy to show us the ropes. They didn't try to sell us or to impress us; they simply tried to help. We learned as much about networking from the manner in which they gave as we did from the invaluable information they disclosed.

So to the follow people, our friends and contributors, thanks for your all of your amazing and generous help! We could not have written this book without you.

Frank Agin, Esq.
Mitch Axelrod
Connie Benesch
Larry Benet
Susan Benjamin
Randy Block
Linda Breakeall
Leland Breef
Kenneth Browning, Esq.
Bob Burg
Stephen Burgay
Adam Christing
Dennis Crow
Hellen Davis
Bernhard Dohrmann
Marty Edelston
Rachel Frishman
Elissa Giambiastini
Adam Giandomenico
Ken Glickman

Jackie Hall
David Hancock
Mark Victor Hansen
C. J. Hayden
Angie Hollerich
Julia Hubbel
Robert Iger
Jeff Kahn
Leonard Koren
Steve Krauser
Ian "Ike" Krieger
Brian Kurtz
Mark LeBlanc
Steve Lillo
Harvey Mackay
Karen McCollough
Sara Michel
Jennifer Morla
Neil Mullanaphy
Andrea R. Nierenberg

Debra Pestrak
Randy Peyser
Robin Ramsey
Caterina Rando
Susan RoAne
Renee Wall Rongen
Paul Rosenzweig
Stanton Royce
Marta Salas-Porras
Darryl Salerno
Dave Sherman
Richard Solomon, Esq.
Barry Spilchuk
Justin Spizman
Marisa Thalberg
Larry Turell
Robert Turell
Melissa Wahl
Kym Yancey
Sandra Yancey

INTRODUCTION

A number of recent publications have heralded networking as the new wonder drug that will enable you to thrive in either a slumping or a booming economy. They give the impression that simply by following a few relatively easy steps, presto chango, you can propel the smallest, most obscure business straight to the top of the Fortune Five Hundred list. Or you could meet the perfect partner, get the ideal job or otherwise strike the mother lode.

First, lets clarify that networking isn't new; it's been around as long as our species. Until recently networking was referred to as being "well connected," having "contacts" or a great Rolodex. It's something we've heard about all of our lives, but with different names. It's an age-old process of exchanging leads, referrals, tips and recommendations; it's mutual support alliances. Whenever someone recommends a restaurant, a travel agent or a book, that's networking. Networking isn't new and it isn't some miraculous potion that you can gulp down at night before bed that will cure whatever ails you by the next morning.

Undeniably, networking is a valuable tool. Reports claim that over 80 percent of all jobs are obtained through networking. Clearly, networking can boost sales and increase profits. It can help you find a wonderful place to live, a great caterer and an endless stream of supportive services that will lighten your load. However, these benefits are little more than byproducts that emanate from something substantially larger and vastly more important.

The essence of networking is surrounding yourself with outstanding, caring and helpful people. It's building mutually supportive relationships with those who will happily help you, it's the process of making and spending time with close friends. Networking is more than a career, marketing or social tactic, it's a way of life. And it doesn't occur overnight! New York attorney Richard Solomon put it best when he said, "The object in life is to be rich in the resource of people." And we agree! Nothing is more important or will enrich your life as greatly as forging close personal relationships, which is what networking provides.

Generosity

When we began this project, we understood that giving was at the core of networking. Everyone told us that to successfully network, you must give; it was the central theme of most books and articles. Oh, how they understated it! Over and over again, the people who we interviewed for this book demonstrated that the essence of networking is more than giving, it's generosity: freely giving on an epic scale that exceeds expectations or needs. This book is a testament to generosity. The word "giving" doesn't do justice to the level of help we received; it doesn't scratch the surface.

Throughout this book we discuss generosity because it is the soul of networking. Generosity is the quality common to all the great networkers we met. They gave instinctively, fully and cheerfully. They were generous in both spirit and deeds. To them, networking meant giving abundantly, often anonymously without fanfare, but with grace and largesse. We found that with generosity also came a warmth, a kindness and a genuine delight in providing help. This was the magic!

As a result, the warmth, helpfulness and generosity that we received far outstripped the rewards we attained from other projects. Besides meeting and getting to know remarkable people, people who we will strive to keep in our lives, we discussed and exchanged views on critical issues. And in the process, it rekindled our occasionally wobbly conviction about the inherent kindness of others.

The best way we know to thank those who have made this book possible is to try to pass the torch. Hopefully in this book we can impress upon you that networking is the building and being part of a community ... a community built on giving generously. It's the art of giving to promote the advancement of others, which uplifts, improves and enriches all our lives and our world. Generously giving triggers the magic, it ignites the responses that will lift you higher, carry you further and take you to places that will surpass your wildest dreams.

★☆★ Action steps ★☆★

We have designed this book to provide more than just theoretical explanations of networking. It has been written to teach you about networking and to show you how to systematically build and maintain your own network. It is stuffed with stories and examples that you can follow and adapt.

At the end of 12 chapters, we have included four action steps that when followed will help you to identify, practice and improve your networking skills. When you have completed a chapter, read each action step and give thought to your answers. There are no right or wrong answers. The purpose of the action steps is to awaken your awareness and to help you develop your networking skills.

When answering the action steps, take your time. Complete one action step per week or proceed at your own pace. Addressing the action steps will reinforce major lessons contained in each chapter and help you customize your network to reflect your unique needs and desires.

Happy networking. Thanks for your interest and enjoy this book!

CHAPTER 1

WHAT IS NETWORKING?

"A network is an organized collection of your personal contacts and your personal contacts' own contacts."
—Harvey Mackay, Author

This chapter will cover:
- ❑ *Defining networking*
- ❑ *Connections*
- ❑ *Diversity*
- ❑ *Reciprocity*
- ❑ *Manipulation*
- ❑ *From the heart*
- ❑ *Fate, coincidence and luck*

The night that Sara and Mark moved into their new home, Patsy and Jay dropped by with containers of take-out food, plastic utensils, a bottle of wine, plastic cups and a large manila folder. They placed the food and drinks on a makeshift table that they fashioned from several unopened cartons, convinced the newcomers to take a well-earned break from unpacking and they all sat down to an inaugural meal.

1

After polishing off dessert, Jay handed the new homeowners the manila folder, which contained a computer disk, four refrigerator magnets and a long list. The list, which Patsy designed, was attractive enough to be displayed on the fridge and the disk could be downloaded to Mark and Sara's computers and synched to their mobile devices. Both the print and electronic versions were laid out in four easy-to-read columns and set forth the categories, names, phone numbers and brief comments about Patsy and Jay's favorite resources. They included the names of restaurants for breakfast, lunch, dinner and take out; doctors; a pharmacy; dentist; veterinarian; market; hardware store; toy store; jeweler; boutiques; photograph developer; nursery; dry cleaner; tailor; shoemaker; plumber; electrician; gardener; computer repairer; handy man; appliance repairer; beautician; barber; babysitters; etc.

Emergencies (Police, Fire and Ambulance)	911
Police (non-emergencies)	555-1212
St. Vincent's Hospital	555-1730

Services

Accounting	Marlena Weinstein	555-1040	Works wonders, most accommodating
Alterations	Stitches	555-7755	Fast and reliable, but a bit costly
Appliance repair	Whiz Kids	555-9300	Fixes anything in the home, reasonable
Auto repair	Northgate Auto	555-0046	Good work, foreign and domestic. Expensive
Baby sitting	Maggie Lloyd	555-3365	Kids love her, but needs lots of notice
Cable TV	Gougers	555-9919	
Computer repair	Fearless Computing	555-7893	Will drop everything in an emergency
Dentist	Alissa Yabara	555-9753	Painless, light touch
Doctor	Lawrence Sklar	555-3000	Great bedside manner. Really cares
Dry cleaning	Maxibright Cleaners	555-6060	Good, fast. Rough on shirt buttons

Electrician	Alvin Shock	555-4121	Excellent work, but in great demand
Gardener	Green Brothers	555-3131	Reliable, but need direction, explain what you want
Home repairs	Manelli Construction	555-7658	Busy, hard to book, but does great work
Housecleaner	Maria Trujillo	555-0981	Thorough, reliable and absolutely trustworthy
Lawyer	Peter P. Frunzi, Jr.	555-4654	Quick to return calls and is sharp
Limo service	Midnight Blue	555-5171	The best we've ever used
Phone company	AT&T	555-3333	
Plumber	Mackey Stickney	555-9922	Gets to you quickly, does a good job, cleans up
Realtor	Lon Murphy & Co.	555-9898	Knows his stuff, fun to deal with
Taxi service	Speedy's Cabs	555-1111	OK. Could use newer cabs
Tree service	Alex's Tree Service	555-8490	Reasonable and leaves everything neat and trim
Yard Work/ hauling	Hall and Hall	555-2136	Excellent for getting rid of all sorts of junk

Food

Breakfast	Willie's Café	555-5511	Best eggs in town!
Lunch	Comforts	555-2300	Great salads, light dishes with oriental flavor
Dinner	Thai House	555-7070	Delicious and inexpensive. Great take out
	Enrico's Ristorante	555-3343	You will think you're in Roma. Fabulous oysters
	Joe's Taco Lounge	555-2233	Good, quick and inexpensive. Try the Lava Soda
	American Pie	555-1919	First-rate burgers and amazing ribs
Major occasions	Chez Mirabelle	555-3331	Trey expensive, but perfect for special evenings
Café	Café de Stijl	555-3737	Great scene, lots of celebs and terrific, light food
Take out	Hot Stuff	555-9876	Always call ahead, the lines are endless

Pizza	Vincent's Pizzeria	555-1492	Delicious thin crust, but they don't deliver
Market	Perfect Foods	555-2527	Fabulous produce and fish. Buy staples elsewhere
Bakery	Savory	555-1909	Heavenly cookies, can't miss with cakes and pies

Immediately, upon receipt of this gift, Sara and Mark had a local network that helped them feel at home in their new home.

Now, think about who you know and, in the space provided below, prepare a list that you could give to someone who just moved into your neighborhood.

_____

_____

_____

_____

_____

What is networking?

Networking is the process of building and maintaining relationships. It's the development of a team that will support your efforts and the efforts of your network teammates to reach your and their goals. In practice, networking is the establishment of multiple informal, loosely-knit, mutual support alliances.

Networking is about forging bonds and sharing. It's connecting with to people who have common interests and objectives and generously giving to one another other. Networking extends into every aspect of your life; it's something you've been doing all of your life. When you recommend a movie, a housecleaner or a personal trainer, you're networking.

We network as soon as we start making our own decisions. As kids, our friends introduce us to the latest and greatest; they turn us on to a constant flow of new friends and information. Rick Frishman's daughter Rachel said she and her friends use networking with "basically everything we do." Rachel was recommended for her job, found a SAT tutor, met guys who she dated and even arranged vacation plans through networking.

Good will is the foundation of networking, it supports and underlies all of your networking efforts. To successfully network you must constantly create good will and then build upon that good will to forge bonds that develop into close, meaningful relationships.

Larry Benet, co-founder of SANG, an author/speakers networking group told us in our interview, "I think, to most people, networking is going to a networking event and swapping business cards back and forth and hoping to meet as many people as they can. I take the exact opposite approach. So, to me, I'm trying to be as strategic as I can when I network and, more importantly, really, just investing into a relationship however best I can.

"I recently met someone who was a speaker who was also from Hollywood, so I went to the event to physically meet him, and then I had a lunch with him, but by finding out what was most important to him—in his case, he wanted to speak more—and so, literally, yesterday, I took a few minutes of my day and I made three email introductions, two to speaker bureaus and one to someone who runs a big event that he might be able to speak at. So, the point is, I just think finding out what is important to someone and seeing if I can't help add some value to hi and contribute to someone in some way, shape, or form."

Networking applies to all areas of life including:

- Friendships
- Romance
- Finances
- Career
- Personal development
- Health and fitness
- Physical environment
- Recreation
- Hobbies and interests

Implicit in networking is the understanding that there will be a giving back, an exchange, "if you do for me, I'll do for you." This unspoken swap of mutual promises underlies networks and keeps them together. Ironically; however, the best networkers are those who give to others because they sincerely love to give and not in order to receive something in return. But that doesn't mean that you don't have to give because even the most giving and generous networkers will eventually stop giving when they repeatedly receive nothing in return.

Networks are not built overnight, they take time, patience and nurturing. Time to meet new contacts, cultivate them and build relationships. Time to discover what your network partners need and to continually try to find opportunities to fully satisfy those needs.

> Networking is a microcosm of life. It's more about how you live your life than what you receive. It's developing expertise, giving, sharing and building relationships. It's the realization that people and generosity are the most important things in life, nothing else comes close, and it's making a dedicated and concerted effort to steer your life in that direction.

Networking is not

"Networking isn't sales and sales isn't networking. They're interrelated, but they're not the same," best-selling networking author Susan RoAne advises. "It's a lifestyle, not a work style. The best networkers don't know that they're networking because for them it's a way of life." Top networkers repeatedly stress that they don't network for the financial rewards, they network because they love helping people and playing matchmaker.

Networking is a marketing tool, a valuable marketing tool that successful people rely upon heavily. However, if you want long-term success, understand that networking requires a sincere desire to help others. You may be personable, you may be clever, you may have exceptional matchmaking skill, but if you're only in it for the money or for yourself, it ultimately won't work. Sure, you might be successful for a while, you might even have a good run, but over the long run, people will catch on and the roof will collapse. So instead of concentrating on increasing your profits, put your efforts into helping others. If you do, the sales will follow as will some other pleasant surprises.

"Sadly, most of us practice transactional networking and we only interact with those who we think we have to in order to complete the transaction," networking coach Sara Michel observes. "We engage our network only when we need to make a sale, find a job or get a lead. As soon as we get what we want, we drop those people off our radar screens and don't talk to them until we need to make another transaction. We become "network users" or engage in, as I like to call it, 'network drive-bys.'"

That said, part of the networking magic is it's creation of converts: individuals who started networking for purely selfish, self-serving reasons often become addicted to performing selfless acts. Although they began networking in order to boost their careers or to further some personal agenda, they're often surprised to find that building relationships, forging friendships, making connections and helping others is infinitely more satisfying. They learn to understand that life is a process and start to place a higher premium on how they live rather than on what they receive.

Networking is not just about you, it's about the group, the network, the collective. It's not about pestering people, manipulating or using them. It's not keeping score, it's not a tit-for-tat or an equal relationship. Networking values effort, it prizes sincere attempts even when they don't achieve what everyone sought.

Rules of the road

Like most disciplines, networking has basic fundamentals that must be fully understood before proceeding further. Although these elements may seem self evident, think about them and don't take them lightly, because they form the building blocks upon which successful networks must be built. Examine how each of these basic rules applies to you, your methods and experiences. Identify how others use them to successfully network and ask yourself if their approaches would work for you? Note all of the areas in which you may be deficient and list steps you can take for improvement.

In this chapter, we will introduce you to the basics of networking. At this time, we only wish to plant seeds and lay the groundwork for material that will be subsequently enlarged upon in this book. The information being provided is intended to stimulate your thoughts and prepare you for discussions in upcoming chapters.

Relationships

Networking is the art of making connections that blossom into strong, mutually beneficial relationships. Although relationships begin with introductions, they hinge on the quality of the connections that are forged. When connections are weak or matches are incompatible, productive networking relationships cannot be built. However, when connections bond, strong relationships can emerge. Bonding and sharing make relationships work.

Kym Yancy, Founder and Chief Marketing Officer and President of e-Women Network, one of the largest networking organizations in the US, told us the best networker is "Someone who is authentic. People really connect with real, and so, the first thing is they are themselves and they are sincere and genuine. At their core, they are others focused. Everybody needs business. We all have needs, but when it comes to networking, you want to be that kind of person whom people are attracted to. Strive to be in other's vortex and energy field because he or she will feel a good vibe from you.

"I know that the people whom I am attracted to in the networking field are the ones who are bright-eyed, friendly, authentic, and they don't come with their agendas. You always know when someone is coming to you with his or her agenda. As quickly as you meet him or her, he or she is trying to figure out how to get to his or her sales message instead of just slowing down and relaxing and just listening and getting into the flow of the conversation and genuinely demonstrating care about the other person and learning more about him or her in a genuine and real way."

When we decided to write this book, we seriously considered calling it *Connections* because connecting or bringing people together for the purpose of building relationships is the essential link needed to successfully network. To make a good connection requires more than a mere introduction; it requires the introducer to think, search, investigate or conduct research into which matches will result in strong, mutually beneficial relationships.

- Without introductions, matches cannot be made
- Without matches, connections cannot be created
- Without connections, bonds cannot form
- Without bonding, relationships cannot be built and
- Without reciprocal relationships, networks cannot last.

When asked about the value of connections, Kim Yancy said, "There are so many things that help to create a connection, but first, it is trying to find some area of common ground. Finding out where there is some kind of common ground or mutual area of agreement, to me, is like a building block for creating connection no matter where you are. I think you start to feel awkward when you are around someone who is not meeting you with that same curiosity and interest in having a connection like you are. Creating a good connection is looking for an opportunity to establish some kind of mutuality that you both can somewhat rally around and, usually, that rally is around saying something nice about that person that helps to establish and start that flow of connection. Once that starts and, if you are with a person who also wants to create a connection, you are off and to the races."

Ideally, the network connections you form will develop into long, fruitful relationships.

Building relationships is the networker's primary objective. Short-term goals such as finding a job, a babysitter or a good sushi bar are secondary goals. Forging strong relationships should be your top priority because they last long after the job, the sitter or hamachi is gone. And network relationships can continually help you find better jobs, more reliable sitters and fresher, more delicious fish.

Answer the following questions:

Are you a good connector? _____ _

If not, why? _____
_____

Do your connections develop into strong relationships? _____

If not, why? _____
_____
_____

Do you know good relationship builders? _____

What can you learn from each good relationship builder?
_____
_____
_____
_____

What steps can you take build better relationships?
1. _____
2. _____
3. _____
4. _____

NETWORING NUGGET

Legendary chef Alice Waters, founder of the four-star restaurant, Chez Panise, is an acknowledged international culinary authority who pioneered the concept of California cuisine. She won The James Beard Foundation's award for outstanding chef and her Chez Panise consistently ranks as one of the top fifty restaurants in the world. Waters has trained, worked with and developed close ties to many of the worlds' great chefs. As a result, her Paris list, has become the food insiders' travel bible. Waters' list includes not only her favorite Parisian eateries, places most of us would never discover, but also contains her tips about shops, markets, and other mouth-watering attractions. Her list has been built on the recommendations Waters has received from her network, which is made up of many of the world's most acclaimed chefs, restaurateurs, food critics, teachers, writers and gourmets. Because of her stature in culinary circles and the extraordinary quality of her network, Waters' list is sought after treasure.

Diversity

In building a network, create a multi-faceted superstructure that includes contacts who possess a wide variety of skills, interests and backgrounds. Fill you life with network members whose help can quickly be accessed so that their assistance will be available to you when you need it.

Visualize your network. Don't picture it as a chain or a single column of contacts who all share similar areas of expertise. Instead, see it as a multi-dimensional meshwork made up of people with

> differing talents, experiences and viewpoints that radiate and link in all directions. Ideally, your network will spread in many directions so it can operate like a blanket to cover any conceivable topic, discipline or target.

Berny Dorhmann is the Chairman and Founder of CEO Space, the No. 5 ranked meeting by Forbes. In our interview, he said, "There are competitive players who are punishing diversity and everything different about us and there are cooperative players who are celebrating all differences and they don't compete and they're the cool companies. Be cooperative and celebrate diversity in your network."

Make your network diverse. Fill it with experts in areas that differ from and compliment your skills. Think of the members of your network as your support team; consider them experts who are fluent in languages you don't speak. Blend a mix of talents, interests, age, gender, race and backgrounds. Besides filling in your gaps, the differences can stimulate, enrich and expose you to knowledge and perspectives that can broaden your life.

NETWORKING NUGGET

Marta Salas-Porras is a graphic designer and multi-disciplinarian with international experience in brand design, product development, and creative strategies with an emphasis on art and technology. When Marta Salas-Porras was a student at Art Center College of Design, the students majoring in differing disciplines seldom mixed. For example, graphic design students and transportation design students kept their distance. Salas-Porras; however, was intrigued by other disciplines and found herself spending considerable time with students from the automotive and industrial design departments. Not only did the processes and materials involved in automotive and industrial design play a major role in shaping Salas-Porras' career, but a student she met from the transportation design department introduced her to his childhood buddy—who she married.

"School and alumni groups are ideal places to begin networking," Salas-Porras advises. "They put you in contact with like minded people who have the same goals as you, who know what you're going through and the hurdles you'll face. Contacts from school and alumni associations can become your friends, mentors, sponsors and advisors throughout your life."

By not diversifying your network, you run the risk of having a group with too many similar skills and areas of glaring weaknesses. You also run the danger of duplicating yourself, of surrounding yourself with "yes" men and women, which undermines a major asset of networks—in influx of fresh, independent support.

How can you diversify your network?

_____

_____

_____

List your weakest areas

_____

_____

Who could help you diversify?

_____

_____

Although it's essential to surround yourself with the best network members that you can reach, be careful not to consider anyone too small or insignificant for membership in your network. There is always a role they can play and you never know what connections people have or what the future may bring. The receptionist who greeted you today, might be the executive assigned to your account tomorrow; the mechanic who services your car may work on the CEO's racing team and hang out with him/her at the track and the kid who delivered your lunch, just might be the bosses child.

Reciprocity

In life, we all try to get things from each other; that's how the world works and has always worked. From ancient times, we have been a people who belonged to tribes and clannish groups. We built societies in which we lived, worked and raised families together. In these societies, each member had specific roles that he/she performed and contributed for the benefit of the group. As a part of life, we gave to and helped each other. And, we also received.

Bob Burg, best-selling Author of *The Go Giver*, said, "Networking is the ability for a person to take their focus off of themselves and put it onto others. It is that person who can move from an 'I' focus or a 'me' focus to an 'other' focus. It is that person who can—this is really what *The Go Giver* was all about in the form of a business parable and it is what *Endless Referrals*, a how-to book, was about—and that is that, when it comes right down to it, all things being equal, people will do business with and refer business to those people they know, like, and trust. So, when you can willingly suspend your self-interests, let us say temporarily suspend your self-interest because we are human beings, we are self-interested creatures and that is fine, there is nothing wrong with that, but when we can willingly suspend that self-interest and focus on constantly and consistently creating value for others, that is when the magic really starts to happen."

Networks operate on similar principles. When it comes to networking, an implied promise exists that "If you help me, I'll help you." This implied promise is the bond upon which networks and societies are built. Without the assurance of reciprocal help, many network members would not give. In networking, reciprocating, returning favors and giving back is not merely expected, it's demanded; it's the price you pay to be a network member.

"In a competitive environment, when we use and exploit each other and take everything we possibly can from network resources, we create a non-sustainable resource that collapses on itself because people feel used," Bernhard Dohrmann, CEO & Chairman of CEO Space International explains, "In a cooperative network, you reward everyone who helps you appropriately for the degree and level of the help received. Sometimes, it's a thank you or a gift and sometimes it's stock, fees or money. There should always be a reward for a contact that made a benefit to you. If you have a benefit, you should give a reward of one kind or another including recognition. Those are sustainable networks that will not collapse on themselves, they will always supernetwork and expand during your lifetime."

Network members are realists. They understand that most requests have more than one motive. They know that the reason given may not be all there is. They also know too well that many good intentioned individuals don't or can't follow through and deliver what they promised. Realists accept the fact that folks get busy, face other demands and simply forget. What they won't abide; however, is repeated, out-and-out exploitation by those whom they have helped because networking involves giving and taking, not exploiting.

- You can't always be the connectee; you must also be the connector.
- You can't always be the taker; you must also give.
- To build a successful network you must be prepared to give at least two or three items for every one you receive.
- Better yet, don't count, just give!

Give generously; don't skimp. If you expect to receive more than you give, you'll be bitterly disappointed. Sure, it you may get away with being a skinflint once, twice or even several times, but sooner or later people will catch on, feel abused and avoid you. And if you get anything, it will be drastically less than you gave and probably more than you deserve.

Train yourself to spot leads or opportunities for your network partners. To identify leads for partners requires you to understand their needs and how these needs can be best filled.

Think of networks as friendships. Your connection to network members is a bond built on the same basic principles as friendship. They are:

- Helping
- Sharing and
- Trusting

Both networks and friendships are intended to be long lasting and enduring, not just fleeting or hit and run contacts. A network, like a friendship, will work only if you're asking, "What can I do for you? It will not work if you're only asking, "What can I get from you?"

Savvy players know that networking fields are seldom level. The rich, powerful and famous are usually better connected and endowed. They have more clout than others, especially newcomers just starting out. So, most beginner networkers must try harder, be more accommodating, more assertive and seize every initiative. Instead of waiting to be asked for a favor from that powerhouse who gave you help, find resources that he/she could use and connect them with your benefactor. To be a good network partner, you must help, help, help. And when you're tired, help some more!

Answer the following questions:

Are you a good reciprocator?

_____

_____

How do you fall short?

_____

_____

How could you improve?

_____

_____

What is stopping you?

_____

_____

Manipulation

Although networkers understand that everyone wants something, they resent being manipulated, used or conned. If, in the list of offenses, forgetting or being too busy to reciprocate is shoplifting, then out-and-out manipulation is murder one and often carries a life-time sentence.

When network members feel used, if they believe that you're only out for yourself, they won't take your calls and they certainly won't help you. Worse yet, they'll tell others about your deceit and once the word gets out, you'll find yourself alone with nowhere to turn.

> Networking requires a delicate balance. People who can help you can also just as easily harm you if you don't deal with them wisely. If they feel that that the only reason you contact them is for what you can get, you'll probably lose a friend, a good contact and your reputation. Even the most altruistic and dedicated networkers won't continue to help those who won't give back. And many of them will tell the world about your duplicity.

Think about your own experiences. We've all had "friends" who called only when they needed something. Remember what it was like when, after not hearing from him/her for the longest time, all of a sudden the phone rings and you're being treated you like his/her closest best friend. These people are users, manipulators, takers. Hopefully by now, we've gotten them out of our lives.

Remember how it felt after you delivered, when the phone calls stopped and your user friend vanished. Didn't you feel used, ripped off and abused? Would you have volunteered to help that person again and subject yourself to further pain?

Well, networks operate in a similar fashion. Just as you distanced yourself from your user friend, network members, even the most generous, will dump those who won't give back. It's basic self-preservation. So if you want to network, it must be reciprocal.

List below how you feel when you speak to people who make you feel like they genuinely want to help.

1. _____
2. _____
3. _____

List below how you feel when you speak to people who make you feel like they have ulterior motives.

1. _____
2. _____
3. _____

From the Heart

The most successful networkers build relationships with others because they love people, the dynamics of relationships and are irrepressible matchmakers. They love sharing their lives and experiences and being closely involved with others. It gives them a sense of community, jointness and purpose. Typically, they're always trying to fix all single people up on dates, send friends to their favorite hideaway resort or introduce them to a cool new acquaintance. The top connectors are "people people" who come from the heart; with them matchmaking is a passion.

Adam Giandomenico, entrepreneur, business developer, and CEO of multiple organizations, told us, "Networking from the heart means building lifelong relationships not only for the sake of building a vast network of people but doing it with the sincere intent of helping others and possibly gaining more than just business contacts. To me, every stranger is a potential new friend. A quality networker recognizes that when you give, you actually receive in kind. Networkers that work from the heart do it for the sake of giving, with no expectation of receiving."

Scores of successful networkers have told us that they derive more joy from building relationships than they do from the ultimate result. They proudly proclaim that they're "networkers" and derive great pleasure from their work. They love nothing more than meeting new people, getting to know them and then connecting them with others.

Networking is built on enthusiasm and passion, which savvy networkers don't fake. Most people can immediately spot fakers, which turns them off and scares them away—and that makes it awfully hard to network.

Most successful networkers usually love:

- People
- What they do and
- Giving of themselves without restriction.

Most successful networkers openly refer those they trust to their resources. To them matchmaking is a game, an opportunity, a calling. They feel that the more solid relationships they help create, the more successful they are. Instead of avoiding opportunities to play matchmaker, they jump at them. In response to requests for the names of contacts, the best networkers immediately real off a few names and then repeatedly inject, "Oh, and also take down the name of _____" and, "Oh yeah _____" and "Then don't forget _____."

Generosity usually pays off because network members will rush to help those who have aided them or members of their network. It's the networker's way of saying "thanks," passing the baton and playing the network game its highest level.

In most cases, it doesn't pay to hide your true agenda. It's usually best to be open and clearly explain exactly what you want. For example, "Can you introduce me to Jack Jones?" If you sense reluctance or misgivings, back off. Everyone has personal limits so don't push or you may turn a potentially good source into someone who avoids you.

When your contact is forthcoming, always express you appreciation and ask how you can reciprocate. Some contacts will be direct and tell you exactly what they expect while others will be silent or noncommittal. If a contact wants a referral fee, clarify in advance how much he/she expects to avoid problems down the road. If he/she is too demanding, express your feelings up front or it will come back to haunt you at a later date.

Trust

Trust is an essential ingredient for successful networks. For networks to succeed, mutual trust is a must! Top networkers will not recommend or extend themselves for those who do not consistently deliver the best; anything less will tarnish their reputations and limit their potential returns. Each member of your network must be completely confident that they can always rely upon you for:

- *Excellent service.* The products or services you provide must be excellent; good or adequate will not be enough. Whatever you provide must shine. It must be memorable and distinguish you from the crowd. Network contacts will be drawn to you because of the high quality of your work. However, if the level of what you deliver falls short, they'll quickly drop you and turn to the next pretty smile. People take pride in dealing with the best. They want the best doctor, piano teacher or house painter and are usually willing to pay for them. Providing excellence distinguishes you and anything less will quickly send you back with the rest of the pack, where it's easy to get lost.

- *Honesty.* Network contacts must know that you will always deliver what you promise. They don't want excuses, they want, and <u>deserve</u>, results. Network partners must be certain that you will give them honest feedback, especially when it may hurt or be awkward. They must unequivocally believe that that you will honor your relationships and not disclose or misuse their confidential information or try to undermine their efforts. In addition, they must be sure that you will not misrepresent or abuse your relationship. If, when you're trying to perform, disaster strikes and everything starts falling apart, inform those who are depending on you so that they can minimize the damage.

- *High standards.* A problem that is rampant in networking is that network members recommend too many people who are not top notch. Often, they lack the standards to know excellence or their recommendation may be to return a favor or make you feel that they are helping you. Other networks spread themselves too thin and try to provide everything to everyone. Recommend only the best people for each particular job. When you're aware of problems with otherwise excellent performers, inform network members regarding their flaws. For example, "John does fabulous work, but he's slow and his projects are invariably late." Being fully informed helps network members make their own decisions, gets you off the hook and enhances your trust quotient.

- *Good fits.* Networking is matchmaking and certain pairings will never create a harmonious fit. We all have unique qualities, values, methods, personalities, styles and objectives, which may not be compatible with those with whom we are matched. The best way to make consistently good matches is to know the people involved, their assets and liabilities, and try to anticipate problems that might arise. Find out the parties' likes, dislikes and basic requirements and when in doubt, ask. Put it straight to them, "What do you want?" And, continue questioning them until you feel you understand precisely what they want.

Qualities That Create Lack of Trust

Not keeping your word

Not showing up

Not giving credit

Routinely being late

Not calling when you promised

Exaggerating

Boasting and bragging

Always putting yourself first

Taking more than your share

Bashing competitors

Not admitting your mistakes

Blaming others.

Always deliver what you promise because it enhances people's trust in you. People buy from and want to be associated with people they trust and people who are trusted by people they trust. They don't like to buy from those who they think are trying to sell them, which is why so many hate the experience of buying a new car. Networks are built on trust and cannot last without mutual trust.

Fate, coincidence and luck

We've called this book *Networking Magic* in deference to the fact that networking often produces baffling and mysterious outcomes. Networking can send us soaring to heights that we might never have scaled by ourselves and launch us off in directions that we never have imagined. The title of this book also conjures up the frequent intervention of events that we can't control, but which we can prepare for, recognize and capitalize on when they occur.

NETWORKING NUGGET

In 1982, Stanton Royce was a single father of children aged eight and three living in a small Ohio Valley steel town. He wanted to find a wife, but realized that his local options were limited. So he created a public relations campaign that he hoped would attract national media attention to his quest for a wife. He invested his meager budget on advertisements in two local newspapers, a billboard and a local radio show that reached West Virginia and Pennsylvania. Sure enough, the local media picked up Royce's story and he received extensive coverage.

A woman in Pennsylvania saw Royce on a Wheeling, West Virginia news broadcast and contacted a friend abroad. Her friend told her coworker about Royce, who told her sister, who introduced him to the woman who became his wife. Royce and his wife, who is a physician and "an incredible person," have now been happily married for over 19 years.

Expect the unexpected. No one knows how things will develop or where they will land. The best-laid plans, the most detailed preparation may fail; the most heartfelt, well-intentioned promises may not be fulfilled. Life, serendipity, the universe, call it what you will, has an amazing way of changing the most well-thought-out plans. When this occurs, and you can be sure that it will, trust your instincts and, when necessary, adjust your focus. When the unexpected strikes, it may be time to move in new directions.

Put your faith in people, ask for their help because they love to help. They love a good story, they love happy endings and when given the chance, will do more than their part to create that perfect ending. When you ask for help, most people are flattered; they feel closer to you and believe that they have an investment in your success.

Put it out there. Give people the chance to help because that's when the magic happens. Wonderful, marvelous, greater than expected bonuses occur when you let your friends in, when you let the world in and when you let the world work its magic. Position yourself to experience the magic. Inform your friends and network partners about your needs and allow them to help.

Adjust your attitude:

- *Be optimistic.* See everything as an opportunity or a step that could lead to a break
- *Be positive.* See everyone as a potential ally, a network partner with whom you can provide mutual help
- *Remain flexible.* No matter how committed or involved you are to a specific strategy, method or approach, be open to its failure and some back-up plans. Like good door-to-door salespeople, carry a number of products in your sample case.
- *Have alternatives.* Realize that other options might be more realistic or productive
- *Be alert.* Don't simply lose yourself so deeply in you endeavors that you can't recognize the warnings signs. Pay attention to those you speak with and learn to recognize danger signs.
- *Monitor developments.* Constantly monitor your situation and make necessary adjustments when appropriate.
- *Be grateful and express it.* Appreciate the efforts of others and make sure to tell them how thankful you are. Actively look for ways to express your appreciation.

Fate, coincidence and luck can also hand you gifts, unexpected bounties, manna from above. Develop your skills, increase your expertise and frequent places filled with rain-makers. Place your self in places and situations where you can demonstrate your talents in the best light to help those miracles along. Keep learning; remain active, involved and productive. If you simply sit around and expect to be discovered, bring plenty of reading material because you may have an awfully long, lonely wait.

A way of life

Networking is more than just a marketing tool; it's a way of life. It's about how you lead you life, not just about closing a deal. Although innumerable businesses have been built through networking, the principles involved are basic. Networking is the building and maintaining of relationships and relationships require caring, helping, kindness, decency, trust and honoring others. In a nutshell networking is about giving and giving generously.

NETWORKING NUGGET

"Hollywood and the motion picture business is all about networking," according to film producer Jesse B'Franklin. "Almost everything in the industry depends on networking. When I first got to LA, I was out four or five nights each week to screenings, parties, book fairs, film festivals, whatever. I needed to meet people, to make contacts and get my name known. Here, people don't ask, 'How are you?' They ask, 'What are you doing?' When my friends get asked out, they never know whether guys are asking them out on a date for romantic reasons or for business reasons."

"You can be sitting in the dentist chair, shot up with Novocain, your mouth stuffed with cotton and the dentist will pitch you for a script he wrote." B'Franklin's husband, director Carl Franklin, decided to cast Don Cheadle in "Devil in A Blue Dress" after they ran into each other and sat interminably in a doctor's waiting room."

"When people ask me how to get a film made, I tell them to go to birthday parties," B'Franklin continued. "I met Billy Bob Thorton and Tom Epperson at a birthday party. As a result of that meeting, they sent me the screenplay they wrote that became *One False Move*. Then at another birthday party, I met Larry Estes, an executive with a company that funded low-budget independent films and through him obtained financing for *One False Move*. To make the movie, I had to find a great director. And I not only found one, but I married him."

The top networkers understand that people and their relationships with them are the centerpieces and the most important assets in their lives. That's why they've built their lives around increasing and maintaining these assets and have wide circles of loyal supporters in their lives.

★☆★ Action steps ★☆★

1. Set forth three steps will make you a better connector.

_____

_____

_____

2. Identify four people who you can enlist to add diversity to your network.

_____

_____

_____

3. List three ways that you can reciprocate for the help others give you.

_____

_____

_____

4. Name three changes you can make to improve your attitude in order to network more successfully.

_____

_____

_____

CHAPTER 2

THE BOARDROOM DINNERS

"All men are caught in an inescapable network of mutuality, tied in a single garment of destiny. Whatever affects one directly, affects all indirectly."
—**Rev. Martin Luther King, Jr.**

This chapter will cover:
- ❏ *Background*
- ❏ *The logistics*
- ❏ *The guests*
- ❏ *The dinners*
- ❏ *The discussions*

Hosting your own

Boardroom, Inc., is a publisher of books and newsletters located in Stamford, Connecticut. It was founded in 1972 by Marty Edelston and is best known for publishing the newsletters: *Bottom Line/Personal, Bottom Line/Health, Bottom Line/Tax Hotline* and *Bottom Line/Tomorrow*. Boardroom hosts monthly dinners that are so inspirational and provide such unparalleled networking opportunities that we decided to devote a complete chapter to them.

27

Boardroom dinners also present an exceptional, easy-to-adapt model that you can tailor and use to substantially boost the quality of your networking and your life.

The Boardroom formula is to surround yourself with remarkable people, the most brilliant, exceptional and accomplished individuals you can find, and to create an atmosphere that will encourage them to share their wealth of ideas, wisdom and experiences. It sounds basic and, in some ways, it is. However, Boardroom has perfected the execution of this idea and elevated it to glittering heights that excite the imagination as well as the guests. The result is networking and human interaction at their pinnacle ... dazzling, stimulating and inspiring experiences that can entertain, teach, uplift and help you build exceptional relationships.

"The dinners are incredible," public speaker and marketing consultant Ken Glickman explained, "Marty brings together such truly amazing people. He creates an atmosphere that encourages people to talk about what they know and the exciting things that are occurring in their area. These evenings create a tremendous amount of enthusiasm and positive energy and besides learning a lot and making great contacts, I always leave with enormous motivation to make something exciting happen. You learn success knowledge, which is the knowledge of how things really work, and the only people who can teach you that are the people who have made things happen. Marty fills the room with those types of people."

As you read about the Boardroom dinners, think how you can host equivalent events on a scale that will fit your budget, needs and your particular circumstances.

Background

Boardroom's publications rely heavily for content on articles and information submitted by the foremost experts and authorities in their fields. This approach is an outgrowth of Edelston's curiosity and his life-long passion to acquire knowledge and understanding. A voracious reader, Edelston was frequently inspired by the books he read so he hired the authors to write articles for Boardroom publications on subjects that fascinated him. He also made a concerted effort to meet and build relationships with the authors of "the best books" and probe their expertise more deeply.

The idea for the Boardroom dinners came after Edelston attended stimulating lunches and dinners hosted by friends and business contacts. He found the guests and the conversations so magical that he decided to try to recapture the experiences by hosting similar events. While compiling the names of potential guests to invite to his dinners, Edelston realized that the experts who contributed to his publications and his existing contacts constituted a fabulous list. So he invited them to his dinners. Since then, he has continued to supplement his list with other experts he meets, hears of or with whom he works.

Originally, Edelston held his dinners in his New York City office, but then he rented an apartment solely to house those events. He hired a great caterer and sent out invitations. Experts attended, met other experts, engaged each other in riveting discussions and enjoyed exciting, enlightening evenings. And no one enjoyed them more than Edelston. Soon, guests told friends about the wonders of Edelston's dinners and as the word got out, the dinners became coveted events and destinations.

Eventually, Edelston's gatherings evolved into the monthly Boardroom dinners that have been held in a private dinning room at New York City's renowned Four Season's Restaurant since 1994. The Boardroom dinners reflect and are a tribute to Edelston's deep curiosity, his thirst for knowledge and his unyielding passion to build relationships with the best and the brightest. They also demonstrate his joy and generosity in sharing with others.

The logistics

Boardroom dinners were co-hosted by Edelston and Brian Kurtz (Boardroom's Executive Vice President) for many years and in recent years Edelston's daughters, Marjory Abrams (Publisher), and Sarah Hiner (President) have co-hosted as well. The number of guests usually ranges between 12 and 27, but 80 people signed up for one special Boardroom dinner. Kurtz believes that groups of 16 to 22 are ideal because seating larger groups is more difficult and tend to make the evenings less intimate. With groups up to 22, ten guests can be seated at both sides of a single, long table with Kurtz and Edelston at either end.

Guests are selected from a database that Boardroom maintains and includes authors who have written articles for Boardroom or individuals who were featured in or interviewed for articles in the company's publications. Other invitees are experts Edelston and Kurtz have met at conferences, meetings or other events and authorities who have worked or consulted with Boardroom. Abrams and Hiner have added their networks to the guest list as well. In addition, guests might have little or no connection with Boardroom other than the hosts' interest in them and their expertise. Selection is geared toward inviting the best people, not toward achieving particular mixes or adhering to any set rules.

Dinners are planned one year in advance and a schedule of the upcoming dinners for the year is sent to those on the invitation database. Out-of-town guests can then plan to attend a dinner during a time when they will be visiting New York or they can arrange trips to coincide with the date of a specific dinner. Each guest sends back reply card, which is enclosed with the schedule, to inform Boardroom of the dinner he/she wishes to attend. Boardroom keeps a list of all responses and as each dinner approaches, confirms the date with each scheduled guest.

An invitation to Boardroom dinners is a hot and prestigious ticket. Besides being invited to dine at one of the world's great restaurants, guests are given the rare opportunity to spend an evening engaged in stimulating conversations with an amazing collection of fascinating experts. Simply being considered to be a guest is exceptionally flattering.

The dinner menu is set in advance, but adjustments are made for guests with specific dietary needs. "The dinners are too special and the people are too special to not accommodate any and all requests. We've even provided car service home for elderly guests," Kurtz noted.

Prior to each dinner, Edelston and the co-host review the guests' biographies and create the seating arrangement. They consider the seating arrangement crucial and strive to make good matches. They strategically seat guests to build upon obvious synergies, which they hope will encourage lively exchanges and the creation of stimulating relationships.

The guests

Guests decide which dinner they wish to attend, so the mix is random and varies from dinner to dinner. Kurtz believes that the randomness and constant changes make the dinners more dynamic. Usually, the guests represent an broad assortment of disciplines, but it can vary. "At one dinner we had six doctors with various specialties, at another we had seven people who were in direct marketing and at yet another, nobody was in healthcare, but six financial analysts attended," Kurtz said. "We could plan it if we wanted to, but by not planning it we end up with something more interesting and always spontaneous."

Since Boardroom places a higher premium on the quality of the guests than on the areas of their expertise, a diverse range of businesses, professions and disciplines have gathered around the table over the years. Guests have been spellbound by information disclosed by experts on everything from terrorism to sex therapy. Medical researchers have explained the latest breakthroughs in their fields and a former White House staffer from the Kennedy White House has shared inside stories about the JFK era.

The dinners

Each dinner is preceded by a cocktail hour, at which time guests arrive, meet one another and mingle. Guests then move to a private dinning room where place cards instruct them where to sit. When the guests are seated, Edelston and/or the co-host welcomes them. Since some guests have attended past dinners, they know why they were invited, but others have no idea. So the hosts explain that the purpose of the dinners is to bring together some of the brightest and most interesting people who can be assembled in one room during one evening and to encourage them to share ideas and information while they enjoy a fabulous meal. "Things that you can ordinarily do on a week night, like going to the movies or the theater are okay, but there's nothing like the stimulation you get spending time with brilliant people." Edelston stresses.

The hosts then go around the room to introduce each guest to the group and inform them about his/her area of expertise. In his introductions, Kurtz finds himself constantly saying that this or that guest "is the World's best _____." Can you think of a better way to spend an evening?

When they are introduced, some guests are asked to share something with the group. For example, what they're most proud of or what they would like to have everybody in the room know about them. Guest may also be asked a probing question such as, "What's new in your field?" or "what are you working on?" However, it's usually better to save lengthy sharing for after the meal.

The hosts try to move the introductory phase along briskly because they want to make sure that all of the guests are properly introduced. However, guests can become so engrossed with information that another guest is sharing or find him/her so interesting that they ask lots of questions, which slows the pace. For example, when a terrorism expert spoke about information he learned at the CIA, the other guests immediately peppered him with so many questions that they stopped everything cold. "When you get great people around the table, the conversations and the dynamics are really mind blowers" Edelston noted. "Fabulous stuff happens." When the intros run long, appetizers are served during while guests are still being introduced.

When the main course is served, the guests have the opportunity to meet, talk and get to know each other. After the main course, salad is served, Edelston rings a chime to get the guests' attention and resume the program. Prior to each dinner, the hosts review information about the guests who are expected to attend and they select stimulating topics to kick off discussions. If eminent physicians are to be in attendance, a good opening might be to ask them what is the latest, most groundbreaking medical research nearing completion in their specialty area. The hosts also try to identify which guests might try to monopolize the room and prepare appropriate responses to bring others into the conversations.

The discussions

The central group discussions begin when one host directs an opening question to an expert. Opening questions are intended to elicit reactions and group participation. Although the expert initially carries the ball, everyone present is encouraged to speak and ask questions. The hosts constantly monitor the discussions to keep them moving and usually let them follow their natural course. However, if a topic plays out or if a guest hogs the floor, one of the hosts will step in and change the subject by posing a question to another guest. Over the years, the hosts have become adept at reading guests' reactions and since they know the guests' bios, they can smoothly move discussions in new directions. As a result, the group rarely stays on one topic for an entire dinner and the conversations seldom stagnate.

"When you have people sitting around a table talking passionately about their areas of expertise and sharing new developments and insider stories, whether it's psychology, cardiology, pending legislation, entertainment, finances or sex, it's simply amazing," Kurtz exclaims. "It becomes a phenomenal evening and you end up learning tons of remarkable stuff in addition to making unbelievable network contacts."

At one time, Edelston recorded the dinners to get story ideas for future Boardroom publications. Although the proceedings are no longer recorded, the hosts inform their guests that they may use information discussed during the conversations as inspirations for future content for their publications. In addition, a member of Boardroom's editorial staff usually attends each dinner to take notes so that staff writers can follow up on good story ideas with guest interviews.

Guests are free to exchange business cards and during the dinner, a list is circulated to get each guest's email address, which will be added to Boardroom's invitation database. After each dinner, Boardroom sends follow-up packages to guests that include samples of its newsletters, one of its new books and a present such as a Boardroom umbrella. A full listing of the guests' contact information and their specialties are also provided with the packages.

In addition, since so many of the guests are authors or experts who have created world class content or products in their areas of expertise, they often offer samples of products they create, or online content. Those "products" are often part of the follow-up package and the follow-up letter has appropriate URL's/websites/links to all of those "goodies" that are not the actual product.

"The people I've met through these dinners are remarkable," Kurtz said. "And having co-hosted these dinners, has taken me to a new level of intimacy with a lot of our guests. Email makes it easy for me to keep in touch with them and I'm always referring people to this one or that one. I've got a great Rolodex and I'm a good networker, but this has expanded my networking well beyond my core competencies."

"When I first started going to the dinners, they made me feel kind of small because I realized how huge the world is and how insignificant each of us is. But now, I've gone completely over in the other direction, which is that the world is such a fantastic place. Everybody is an expert in something and when you can share your expertise and your passions in a way that is totally giving, extraordinary things occur," Kurtz added. That's networking magic!

Host your own

The moral of the Boardroom story is to surround yourself with remarkable people. You owe it to yourself and those you love to meet and build relationships with the best. Nothing can improve your life like associating with terrific people; it gives your life fullness. And, remember, when you build relationships with extraordinary individuals, you also become privy to their networks, which are usually composed of equally outstanding people.

So shoot for the stars, the top, the highest rung you can reach. However, in the process, don't abandon your present cronies and network partners. Add new faces, new spice, new minds and new ideas, but also don't forget or abandon the old.

Take the initiative and put yourself together with those who can stimulate you, excite you, teach you, broaden you and make the nights fly by. Top people are frequently open to new experiences and new relationships. Some may initially say no to your approaches, but there is always tomorrow and if your dinners, or gatherings or whatever you do build good buzz, they'll be clamoring for an invitation.

Berny Dorhmann told us, "In today's world, networking has changed so much. You have to, as never before, build relationships. Networkers who route things quickly to meals make deals. We think meals make deals—but it's really about linking lives. The faster your networking gets to meals—a no host, separate checks meal—I think the quicker your relationship can move."

Naturally, we all can't host lavish dinners at the Four Seasons or draw from the same remarkable talent pool as Boardroom. How many people would fly in to your town and build a trip around one of your dinners? Yet, we can all start small gatherings filled with the most exceptional people we know and then build.

Start with the best people you can reach. Invite your most interesting, enjoyable, entertaining friends and contacts. Invite people you've heard about, but don't know. Invite people who you've wanted to meet. Select guests who are experts in fields that interest you and in areas that you know nothing about. It doesn't have to be all talk. If you know musicians, poets or entertainers ask them to in order to refresh the mix.

Work on a scale that you can afford. Although good food certainly helps, great people should be your top priority. So when you're starting out, think first about the quality of your guests, about attracting the very best people. And if the food is a way to attract heavy hitters, do whatever you can, within your means, to get them to the table. Then get them talking.

Prepare and ask questions that will make your guests expound. Once they're talking, sit back and let the magic work. Only interject if a guest filibusters, gets too far off course or the discussion becomes dry. Then steer the conversation gently by asking another question that could ignite more stimulating talk.

Once you get rolling, do it right. Kurtz recommends sparing no expense, "And if that means doing fewer dinners, but making them all 'perfect,' I would recommend that."

The Lasting Legacy

Years after we interviewed Bryan Kurtz for the first edition of this book, we revisited the topic of The Boardroom Dinners and Martin (Marty) Edelston with him.

Bryan Kurtz told us, "The Boardroom Dinners are still going strong—and they are actually better than ever. We have even made some improvements and those were incorporated into this new edition. It is very rewarding that this is still a model that is easy to replicate and it is one of the best ways to treat the most important people in your network so they truly become a community.

"Marty Edelston, the inventor of the Boardroom Dinners, passed is an entrepreneur's entrepreneur. His career is one making a huge difference to millions of consumers through the publications and books he created. He has saved lives, businesses and careers. The stories are endless. I guess the moral is that there's a lot you can accomplish when you read everything and are always willing to get involved.

"Marty is a man of the highest integrity, he's got a quick wit, he's got more intellectual curiosity than anyone on the planet and the biggest heart to boot. To know Marty is to love him...but that doesn't mean he's a pushover either. He always challenges you to be better than you ever imagined you could be. He's taught (and still teaches) anyone who will listen to always strive to be 'the world's best' and to only surround yourself with others who strive to do the same.

"Marty will tell you to this day that he is just an ordinary guy who has been able to do extraordinary things because he has never lost his desire to learn and grow. An amazing work ethic and a need to make a real difference with people was a big part of it too—you don't publish the country's largest consumer newsletter and stay in business for over 40 years without some very special qualities. He's special but he will never tell you that himself. His legacy as a true American entrepreneur and hero lives on today and will live on forever."

★★★ Action steps ★★★

1. State three ways you could adapt the Boardroom dinners to work for you.

_____

_____

_____

2. What you would like to accomplish by hosting your events?

_____

_____

_____

3. Who would you invite to your events?

_____

_____

_____

4. What new features would you add to your events?

_____

_____

_____

CHAPTER 3

BUILDING YOUR NETWORK

*"The quickest way to the top
is to take everyone with you."*
—Bernhard Dohrmann, Ceo &
Chairman Of Space International

This chapter will cover:
- ❏ *Focus*
- ❏ *Taking inventory*
- ❏ *Listening*
- ❏ *Helping*
- ❏ *You are your product*
- ❏ *Start close to home*
- ❏ *Identify hurdles*
- ❏ *Promises, promises*

If you want to succeed, build a great team. A great team multiplies your prospects for success; it enables you to form relationships with powerful people who can make your dreams come true. A great network supports your strengths, fills in your weaknesses and allows you to trade and build on your teammates' accomplishments. When you have a great team, people assume that you are great and will stand in line to get to know you, do business with you and help you. They will also be delighted to pay your price.

Okay, so you understand the value of a strong network. Now, how do you build a great network, how do you get started?

Well, unless you've been living in total seclusion, you already have a network in place. And your network is probably more extensive than you realize. It may not be a great network yet, but it's a beginning, a place from which to build. Your network most likely consists of your family, friends, schoolmates and business associates. It includes people with whom you've conducted business, socialized or otherwise interacted. In addition, **the members of your network members' networks are also members of your network**. Therefore, if your accountant is a member of your network, so are all the members of your accountant's network.

NETWORKING NUGGET

When Johnny Carson was preparing to leave the Tonight Show, the candidates to succeed him boiled down to Jay Leno and David Letterman. At the time, Leno was regularly going on the road to perform his comedy act in cities throughout the country. Letterman, on the other hand, remained in the New York City area and concentrated on his show.

According to industry sources, in every city where Leno performed, he called the local NBC affiliate stations and said, "Hi, this is Jay Leno. I'm in town this week. If you would like for me to pop by your studio for an interview or to entertain your staff for a few minutes, just plug me in." He also befriended station executives and invited them to his concerts.

Just before it was time for NBC to decide on the permanent Tonight Show host, Leno called his friends at the affiliates and asked them to put in a good word for him with NBC. In turn, the affiliates contacted the network and said, "Go with my friend Jay Leno!" Insiders tell us that the power of Jay Leno's "network networking" helped him get one of the most coveted and high-profile jobs in television.

To build great networks, you need great people: great lawyers, doctors, dentists, accounts, insurance agents, friends, etc. If a disaster arose in the middle of the night, who would you call? Can you count on him/her? Would he/she solve your problem? If a disaster arose in the middle of the night, who would call you? How could you help? Could they count on you?

If you want to build a great network, you must continually expand and upgrade your existing network. Everything always changes and what constitutes a great network today, could be less than great tomorrow. Network members drop out and lose interest: they change businesses, interests and their lives and so will you. In networking, expanding and upgrading is a never-ending process: heads of states, CEOs, established leaders at every strata of society are constantly seeking to find the best people and incorporate them in their networks, add them to their teams. So the process of expanding and upgrading never stops; it's what building a network is about.

To expand and upgrade your network requires focus. Once you realize that you have a network, it's time sharpen your focus and begin to see with new eyes. Continually look for new and better network members and search for links that tie your network members with virtually everyone you meet and everything you experience. Search for opportunities for your network members and help them reach their goals.

Follow the example of the successful people in your life. Have you noticed how frequently they take new information and relate it to their particular area of expertise? After hearing stories, reading articles and having new experiences, they immediately tie them to their specific areas of interest. Often, it seems as if they're explaining it to themselves, exploring the full ramifications of the new information and examining how to incorporate it within their own particular context.

Have you observed that writers tend to see everything as material for potential stories, financiers always look at the bottom line, publicists think about promotional possibilities, comics turn everything into humor, lawyers probe for hidden liabilities and medical workers zero in on health?

Well, successful networkers operate on the same principle. They're obsessed with connections with and instinctively search for them. Accomplished networkers see the world in terms of leads, contacts and opportunities that will bring them closer to network relationships. They view the world optimistically and see every possibility as an opening that could lead them to their pot of gold.

Examine how the successful people you know process new information. Then apply their methods to your situation.

Awareness

Focus starts with awareness. Usually, it's a painless process that is a natural byproduct of our interests and it occurs without planning or effort. When we are truly interested or involved, doors open through which we can see. How many times after being introduced to something new, have you found yourself merrily breezing along when suddenly, your antennae pick up signals that alert you to information about that subject … a subject in which a just short time ago you had little or no interest. Before long, everything concerning that subject seems compelling, is lodged in the forefront of your mind and everything relates to it.

Isn't it amazing that as soon as you buy a car, you notice how many identical models are on the road? It's not that those models weren't there before; after all they didn't all just simultaneously race out of the showrooms. They were probably out there for a while, but you simply didn't register seeing them. Now that you're aware, you see them everywhere.

The same holds true for networking. In most cases, your contacts have been around for quite a while. However, you confined them to specific niches. To you they were friends, family, business associates or service people, not potential network contacts. When you expand your awareness to see those around you also as members of your network, you can refine your networking focus.

Focus on networking. Practice honing your networking focus until it becomes a highly-developed skill. Begin by:

- Asking yourself if people you know, meet or hear about could help you network.
- Clarifying precisely how these people could help. For example, introduce you to the mayor, recommend you for the membership in the garden club or inform you where they found their antique Venetian carnival masks.
- Find out what places and events would be worth attending to expand your contacts.
- Question how you can make the best use of information to connect you with your targets.

Developing networking focus isn't difficult and before long, it will become second nature. Work to get it down pat because the ability to sharply focus is a priceless skill that will bring you rewards for the rest of your life.

Listening

Learn to listen and observe. Let others carry the conversation and while they do, pay careful attention to what they say. If you let them speak, most people will be revealing. Thy will disclose who they are, what they do and what they need. And, if after listening, you're still not sure, ask them directly. Show your interest; be attentive.

In our interview, Adam Giandomenico said, "Edgar Watson Howe once joked, 'No Man would listen to you talk if he didn't know it was his turn next.' It is unfortunate that this is true in the way many approach the art of communication. They are so busy formulating their responses in their heads that they hear but don't really listen. Listening is the first role and responsibility of a networker.

"When building your network, it is vital that you are able to establish a common denominator, which allows you to build mutual credibility between you and the other person. To accomplish this, you must listen and reply specifically to the subject matter that the other person is talking about.

"This type of listening and response will solidify a positive first impression and will also allow you to figure out if this person is a good match for your network. Listening is the first step in building the foundation of a potential long-term relationship."

Try to remember their names and repeat it in your conversations. It shows that you are attentive and it makes conversations warmer, more personal … but don't overdo it or it doesn't ring true. When you're attentive, those who you're with will be flattered. They will consider you to be one of the most interesting people they know. People are eager to spend more time speaking with good listeners and will reveal information and insights more quickly.

When the conversation turns to you, answer briefly and then turn it back to the other person. Let him/her be expansive. Ask questions that will encourage them to continue. When you're with interesting people, listening is fun. After we all know, who we are and what we've done, but we don't have the same knowledge about others. Listening is the best way to find out and to make strong connections.

Taking Inventory

Your network inventory
Sharpen your focus by making a written list your network members. Don't overlook anyone! Make your network broad and all-inclusive. Titles and

positions can be deceptive and not indicate an individual's abilities, connections or value to your network. Include people who you like and whom you enjoy being with and being associated with.

NETWORKING NUGGET

As automotive marketing guru James Ziegler was waiting for a flight at Atlanta's Hartsfield Airport, Leo Mullin, former CEO of Delta Airlines, was with a group being photographed for Delta's magazine. Ziegler had always wanted to meet Mullin, but he resisted the temptation to introduce himself since Mullin was obviously busy.

A short while later, Ziegler noticed Mullin walking with Bill, a blue-collar mechanic for Delta, a friend of Ziegler's from his adult Sunday school class. Earlier that day, Ziegler had bumped into Bill and said hello, but it never dawned on him that Bill was with Mullin. A few minutes later, Mullin walked over to Ziegler and introduced himself. He and Ziegler talked for about twenty minutes and exchanged business cards before Mullin returned to the photo shoot.

Shortly thereafter, Bill came by. Only then did Ziegler remember that several months ago, over coffee, he mentioned to Bill that he would really like to meet Mullin. Bill never indicated that he knew Mullin and Ziegler didn't realize that Bill had access to him. Since that day at the airport, Ziegler has had a direct link to Mullin. Although he has never contacted Mullin to leverage the relationship, he occasionally sends him complimentary notes to report that he received outstanding service from Delta employees. Ziegler says that he would have no hesitation contacting Mullin, when appropriate, and believes that he could count on Mullin's help.

On your list, write next to each name the reason you included that person on your list. Be specific.

Generally, those you list will fall into two categories:

1. *Direct contacts (First generation contacts).* People who have what you want and can give it to you directly. For example, your objective may be courtside tickets at Madison Square Garden, the names and contact information for media that cover fabric design or a meeting with your U.S. Senator. On your list, write down your precise objective.

2. *Intermediary contacts (Second generation contacts).* Those who can introduce you to or influence others who actually have, can deliver or lead you to your objective. Intermediaries usually can't deliver your ultimate objective, but they can make introductions, write recommendation letters and move you closer to your destination.

Your personal inventory

Next, inventory your personal assets to identify what you can bring to the table and to learn what you really want. To find your personal assets, think about all the things you do well and enjoy doing, classes or training you've taken, awards you have won, jobs held, skills learned, accomplishments achieved and clients/customers satisfied. Don't overlook "intangible" qualities such as determination, people skills, capacity for hard work, honesty, reliability, humor, kindness, taste, sensitivity and compassion.

Identify your talents, skills and values. Your:

- Talents are your natural attributes. Some lucky souls sing beautifully, while others can dunk a basketball or mentally calculate long rows of figures
- Skills are the capabilities that you acquired: Web site design, fine-furniture making or antique bookbinding.
- Values are the objectives that you consider important: high earnings, creativity, recognition or working in teams.

Remarkably, few people can identify talents, skills or values even though they play a crucial role in their behavior. When you approach people, they're interested in benefits; they want to know what you can do for them. If you've identified your talents and skills, you can more clearly articulate the benefits that you can provide and see how it fits into different situations. Instead informing a network contact, "I'm an office administrator," you can explain that you can keep a business running smoothly by handling hiring and firing, staff supervision, scheduling, ordering, bookkeeping and billing.

The most important factor in building strong relationships is that the parties share common values. According to Career Transition Coach, Randy Block, "The most important linkage in a networking situation is that you and your network partners share congruent values." Think about it; it makes good sense. People prefer to deal with those who share their values. For example, if you like stability, working under pressure, heated competition or living on the edge, you're probably going to be happier being with those who feel the same.

Bob Burg indicated in our interview, "People look to connect with people whom they think will add value to their lives. Value is the relative worth or desirability of a thing to the end user or beholder. In other words, what is it about this thing, this product, service, concept, idea, opportunity, or person that brings such value or worth to another person that they want to invest in that person whether it is money, in terms of buying their products or services, or whether it is time, in terms of a connection. Value tends to manifest itself in five general ways: excellence, consistency, attention, empathy, and appreciation. Those people who are able to communicate those what we call 'elements of value,' those are the people who tend to make the strongest connections with others."

In the past, values were seldom discussed. However, when people who are connected share common values, bonds can be forged that can lead to strong, productive relationships. Common bonds make relationships work; they put people on the same page. So, if you're trying to make a good match, focus on the other party's values.

Think about your values. Look back on situations in which you had fun, were happy, successful, proud and made money. What did you like most about them and would like to replicate?

When you've identified your talents, skills and values, you will feel more confident because you recognized precisely what you have to offer and the values that make you happy. Your self-knowledge and confidence will increase your ability to clearly communicate, which will boost your appeal. Instead of vaguely asking network contacts if they know of job openings, your approach will be stronger when you say, "This is what I'm good at, these are the benefits I provide. Do you know of anyone who can use my talents?"

Helping

"Helping is the best form of networking," Stephen Burgay, Vice President of marketing and communications at Boston University advises. "The key to building a network is establishing good relationships with your network members. You need to get to know them and wherever possible, help them out long before you need them to help you." If you help, those you helped will pick up your call and they will be more willing to assist you.

The ideal time to build your network is when you are in a position to help others and you don't need their help. Or as President John F. Kennedy advised, "The time to repair the roof is when the sun is shining." Burgay calls this "implicit networking" because you have no agenda. In contrast, "explicit networking is when you have an agenda such as needing a job, wanting to change jobs or being on the move."

Implicit networking builds good will and can position you for tomorrow. Help others whenever you can because it might motivate them to assist you when you need help. For example, if you have a job, assist whomever you can and don't worry about receiving anything from them in return. If you lose your job, you may want to call upon those you helped. Had you not helped them, they may be less inclined to assist you since you're no longer in power. However, they may fulfill your request in gratitude for past favors. Usually, you need networking most when you're no longer in a position of power. So give early to build relationships that transcend changes in your circumstances.

To build your network, give your product or perform your service for free to the right people. Establish yourself by not charging important contacts, those who can launch your career. Write it off to good will; consider it an investment. Usually, people are more willing to try things that are free and will remember when they receive something of value, especially when it comes at no cost. The object is to get your product or service out there, to let its quality speak for itself and to impress those who are in a position to help. If it's really good, your contacts will spread the word and endorse you, your product or service.

Give generously and gladly. Give more, not less, than is expected. Don't just fill expectations—exceed them—exceed them beyond your contact's hopes. Give your all. Build a reputation for generosity and magnanimousness; make the grand gesture. Never give resentfully or sullenly as if your arm was being twisted; always be gracious. Don't brag or broadcast your generosity to others or repeatedly remind those you helped of your largesse.

Be generous in spirit and deed and, when possible, be anonymous. Create an example of generosity that others will admire and be encouraged to follow. Giving generously and gladly can create a circle of helping, giving and sharing that will assist others and that you can remain a part of long after your power and influence have waned.

Get organized

Now that you've identified the members of your network, create a system that will always keep you current. Create a detailed network database on your rolodex, mobile device or address book or simply start a separate card or computer file. Also investigate the numerous computer programs that provide contact-organizing services. They include ACT!, Goldmine and tons more. Think of the members of your network as your stock in trade, your inventory. Keep detailed records of your stock of network members and review them regularly.

Collect as many names as possible because you never know when a contact could be or lead you to the perfect fit. Successful networks collect business cards and contact information as if it was money. They believe you can never have too many. A contact who you barely met, may have heard about you, been impressed by you or think that you or your product/service are fabulous and want to hook you up with his/her network.

Divide your database into three groups.

- *A Group*—Your top, most important network members. The people who you feel will help you the most.
- *B Group*—Other, less important contacts who you have actually met and
- *C Group*—People you don't know but have heard of, seen, read articles by and would like to meet.

At a minimum, your database should contain the contact's:

- Name
- Business/Employer
- Street address
- E-mail address
- Telephone number
- Back up telephone numbers
- Fax number
- Specialty area
- Source information such as how you got his/her name, how and where you met, and friends, associates and interests that you may have in common.
- Personal information including your conversations with the contact, the subject and ultimate result of those conversations, requests you made, previous help given, dates you last spoke and the results and notes on the contact's family, birthday, families' birthdays, hobbies and special interests and/or achievements including those that may have received media attention.

Become a collector. Gather lots of information about your contacts and note it in your records. This information can be the icebreaker that softens contact and makes him/her want to help. It can also assist you in positioning yourself. For example, when you know that an elusive contact is a breeder of champion pugs, your might want to read up on pugs attend some dog shows.

Get into the habit of collecting business cards and making notes. Carry a small notebook or a personal digital assistant, such as a mobile device, at all times to record names and pertinent information. Keep notebooks and writing implements in you car, briefcase, purse, boat, and near all computers and phones.

Ask everyone you meet for his/her business card and give them yours. On the back of their card, jot down where and when you met them and what you discussed. Each night, when you empty your pockets, briefcases or purses, toss the cards into a receptacle that you assign exclusively for your collection of contact information. Then set aside a specific time each week, like 9 AM each Monday, to transfer information from the cards to your network database.

Review and update your network database on a regular basis. Update all changes as soon as they occur. At the least, scan your database once a month and go over it from top to bottom every three months. The more familiar you are with your list, the more easily and quickly you will be able to link network contacts when the need arises.

You are your product

Regardless of what service you provide or product you produce, remember that you are your product. In networking, you are always on stage. People will watch you with a critical eye and take notice of how you act. If people like and believe in you, they will extend themselves on your behalf, they will speak highly of you to others. People who trust you will give preferences to you, your products or services; preferences that will make your life much easier and your profits much greater.

However, if people don't like, believe in or trust you, they won't help you. They may not say "no" to your face, but when it comes time for them to deliver, something will always divert them and you won't get what you want. And once doors close, they become much harder to reopen.

Name recognition can be important in building and maintaining a great network. Become a celebrity, an expert or a well recognized authority. People remember celebrities and expert authorities. Position yourself so that when your name is mentioned, others will instantly think he/she's the best wills and estates lawyer, the top tennis coach or the finest jazz singer. Network contacts like to be associated with well-known people; it enhances their stature and gives them bragging rights.

Start locally. Move from your street, to the neighborhood, the town, county, state, national and the world. Build a solid support base and continue to branch out. When you venture into bigger and deeper waters, maintain and keep in contact with your base

Nearest and dearest

In building your network, it usually makes sense to work from inside out. When possible, build initially upon those who are nearest and dearest to you. Then inch your way toward others who aren't as close. First lay a foundation of those who:

- Are closest to you and who know you best
- Have the best connections
- Can provide or bring you closer to your objective.

Those who are closest to you usually have the best knowledge of your talents and skills. They have witnessed and know first-hand about the level of your abilities and are generally happy to recommend you to their contacts. When they vouch for you, their opinions may hold great weight and be immediately accepted without further proof or documentation. And, their knowledge of your strengths and weaknesses gives them insights regarding whom they should match you with and who would make the best fit.

Close contacts, especially family and dear friends, often have a high stake in your success and will go to greater lengths to link you up with contacts who can help. Often, your near and dear ones will be more willing to go out on a limb for you, contact powerful people or call in chits that they've obtained in return for past favors. In addition, they might recommend other helpful contacts or strategies.

Be expansive; define your "nearest and dearest" liberally. Don't look only to your parents, siblings and close friends. Contact your aunts, uncles, grandparents, distant relatives, in laws, godparents, business associates and members of their families. Explore all connections. Ignore the "removed" with relatives who are "once removed." With friends, call upon their parents, siblings, relatives, friends and business associates. Leave no source unturned.

Remember that

- The easiest and most efficient way to expand your resources is to tap into your sources' resources and
- The smartest place to start networking is with those who love or owe you.

So whenever possible, begin your networking close to home. Develop a plan, have patience, build a solid foundation and work from there.

Teachers, bosses and colleagues

Your teachers, bosses and business associates also know and can attest to your strengths and abilities. And, they often benefit from your success. When you progress, it's a reflection on those who taught you; when you succeed, it makes your mentors look good and enhances their stature and credibility. If you become a major success, they can become minor celebrities.

Teachers, bosses and business associates, past and present, have extensive and valuable contacts. They usually pinpoint who to call, when to call and what to say. People in the know can often accomplish more in one phone call than you could do in years working on your own.

NETWORKING NUGGET

In his marvelous book, *Dig Your Well Before You're Thirsty*, Harvey Mackay relates TV personality Pat O'Brien's networking story.

At the University of South Dakota, O'Brien was a student of Dr. William O. Farber, chairman of the Political Science Department and a master networker. Since South Dakota is so isolated, Farber decided to build a network that would help his students extend their reach so they could reach their full potential. In his network, Farber joined forces with powerhouses including Al Neuharth of Gannett Company, Inc. (founder of *USA Today*), Robert Swanson, CEO of Greyhound, Del Webb and General Mills, Phil Odean, CEO of BDM, Ken Bode of *Washington Week in Review*, U.S. Senator Tim Johnson, former Senator Larry Pressler and two federal judges.

When O'Brien told Dr. Farber that he was interested in pursuing a broadcasting career after graduation, Farber contacted another former student, Tom Brokaw. Brokaw was then the news anchor at the NBC affiliate in Los Angeles and made one phone call that got O'Brien a job at NBC in Washington, DC. Two-days after being a student in South Dakota, O'Brien was working for David Brinkley, a giant of news broadcasting, in the nation's capitol. Because of networking he was able to launch his long, highly successful career in broadcasting.

Observe and file

As you learn to focus, teach yourself to become more observant. Push yourself to look closely, listen and be more precise. Top networkers are keenly observant and are wonderful listeners. They pay close attention to what they see and what is said. They ask questions and make concerted efforts to get names and facts right.

With names and facts learn to always be precise.

- Ask for the correct spelling of every name, even those that are common. When you're given a name, the best approach is to ask, "How do you spell that?" Then write it down and repeat the spelling aloud.

- Double or triple check all numbers including telephone numbers, addresses, statistics and especially monetary amounts. When leaving you phone number or email address with voice mail or a message taker, clearly recite the number/address twice.

- When you give any contact information over the phone, be clear and precise. If you have a name or address that is difficult to pronounce or spell, find a way to articulate it clearly. If you say "A as in ____" select an example that is unusual like "alligator or artichoke," not a more common work that is more likely to be confused

- Add a signature file at the bottom of each email that sets forth your name and contact information. You can also add a business slogan or message to your signature file.

> Successful networkers are attentive, ask meaningful questions and seldom interrupt. They let the conversation center around the other person and don't try to steer it in other directions. Networkers know and capitalize on the fact that most of us feel more comfortable speaking with to those who give us their full attention.

When accomplished networkers receive new information, the wheels immediately start turning. Automatically, they mentally catalog every name, every story, every event and every statistic. Then they instinctively scan their list of contacts for possible links. Occasionally, obvious connections leap out, but most of the time, the new data is simply noted and placed on hold for future use.

While they are taking in and connecting information, savvy networkers continue to look you straight in the eye, listening attentively and asking good questions. It's not that they're insincere or manipulative; it's just highly refined multi-tasking, the art of doing several things simultaneously and doing them well.

Identify hurdles

Before you begin to network, examine possible roadblocks that could block or delay your success. At each networking stage, anticipate what could derail your efforts or prevent you from reaching your goal. List all that could go wrong. For example, before you call a potential target, plan what you would do if he/she refuses to take your call. Should you send a note, email or sit on his/her doorstep? Should you ask another network contact to call or should you just abandon your efforts and your attention to another target.

Adam Giandomenico told us, "In Cervantes' book *Don Quixote of La Mancha*, the main character sings about his quest for the impossible dream, the unreachable star. In the story, he kept moving forward on his quest regardless of what people around him said. You will find parallels in networking. Reaching the unreachable is only true if you allow it to be so.

"If you carry within you a strong belief in what you stand for, and are persistent and fearless in your endeavors, even the most unreachable can be within arm's length and all you have to do is reach out. That is really what networking is about. Networking is reaching out to others with the purpose of finding out how you and the other people in the room can build a mutually beneficial relationship. In business as in life, no man is an island. At one point or the other, we all need a helping hand, and being that helping hand at the right time and the right place can make all the difference."

Identifying possible hurdles enables you to easily handle many of them when they arise. It also can alert you to problems or insurmountable flaws in your plans before you've spent time, effort and energy or embarrassed yourself. Anticipating obstacles can also force you to develop more realistic or more feasible strategies. Finally, it can help you determine what additional assistance you may need and how much that assistance is worth to you.

Promises, promises

Most people mean well. When you're together, they're warm, friendly and brimming with encouragement, compliments and helpful advice. They have a million ideas as to what you should do and how you should do it. Some may reel off the names of your heroes and claim that they are closest buddies. They may even volunteer to call someone at the top of his/her field, which would put you on the map and solve all your problems. Well, don't hold your breath!

Some people are merely big talkers or shameless name droppers. Usually, the name droppers are easy to spot. When most contacts make promises to you, they will sincerely want to help. However, other pressures and demands have an uncanny way of disrupting the best of intentions. Unfortunately, the old saying, "out of sight, out of mind," is frequently true and many contacts, no matter how sincere or well-meaning, simply don't come through.

So take every promise with a grain of salt, not as a guarantee or sure thing. Give it the same weight as you would a stock tip from a stranger. Until proven to the contrary, accept that your contact's promise was well intentioned and made with a true desire to help. Build on his/her good intentions. Salvage something positive from your contacts' promises and from their failure to deliver, but never show annoyance or irritation. Don't try to shame or blackmail those who failed you into helping you. They will resent it and your methods can easily backfire.

In the face of disappointment, work to keep open the avenues of communication with your contacts, strive to build good will and position yourself to fight another ... and hopefully, more productive ... day.

★☆ ★ Action steps ★☆ ★

1. List the names of five direct contacts and state reason you listed each.

_____

_____

_____

2. Provide the names of five intermediary contacts and state the reason you listed each.

_____

_____

_____

3. Identify below your talents and skills in the order in which you're most proficient. Think in terms of benefits that you can provide rather than job titles or descriptions.

_____

_____

_____

4. State your values in the order of their importance below:

_____

_____

_____

CHAPTER 4

IDENTIFY YOUR TARGETS

"I'm always looking for people
who do a better job than I can."
—T. Boone Pickens

This chapter will cover:
- ❑ *Types of introductions*
- ❑ *Identify your purpose*
- ❑ *Compelling vision*
- ❑ *Identifying people*
- ❑ *Prioritize*
- ❑ *Shoot for the top*

Networking starts with introductions and introductions come in a number of forms. For the purposes of this book, we have separated them into five categories:

- Cold calls
- Leads
- Cold introductions

- Warm introductions and
- Personal introductions

Cold calls are attempts to contact people who you don't know and have little or no information about. They can hardly be called introductions. Calling names that you received from telephone directories or similar listings are cold calls. They are usually attempts to contact targets who you don't know without any introduction or referral. Most of those irritating, impersonal phone solicitations we all receive are cold calls.

Leads, as used in this book, are names that usually fit a common profile, such as men between ages 25 and 35; self-employed carpenters or mothers with more than three children. Those who give you leads may not know the people included on lead sheets or list. Frequently, the names on lead sheets are compiled by list services and similar sources. For the purposes of this book, leads are simply names without any other type of referral. When you contact a lead, it's little more than a cold call.

Cold introductions are more personal leads. For example, when your friend Bill tells you to, "Call my cousin Sally, she may be looking for someone like you." Get permission from Bill to mention to cousin Sally that he/she suggested you call or else your call will have the same meager impact of a cold call from a stranger. Without Bill's permission, your call is little more than a lead.

Warm introductions occur when Bill phones cousin Sally and tells her that you will be calling. If Bill praises you, his introduction will be even warmer. Warm introductions usually give you a better more enthusiastic reception and it may spur Sally to jump the gun and call you. Warm introductions give you immediate credibility and cousin Sally is likely to accept what Bill recommends. So when a contact gives you a lead or a cold introduction, ask if he/she could call first to turn it into a warm introduction.

Personal introductions occur when Bill personally introduces you to cousin Sally. He may arrange for the three of you to lunch together, bring you to Sally's office or introduce you at an event. Warm introductions carry the message that "this is someone good, someone you should know or use." Therefore, they are the most desirable introductions and what you should try to obtain.

Identify your purpose

Before selecting targets, clarify in your mind exactly what you want. Be specific. Do you want to find someone who can help get your kid into Harvard, do you want to hire a wedding videographer who also takes still, black and white photographs or do you want to learn how to start an organic garden with drip irrigation? When you are not completely clear about your purpose, you can't explain what you want to others.

NETWORKING NUGGET

In June 1974, when Rick's friend Bob Igar from Ithaca College was a weatherman in Ithaca, New York, he went to New York City to look for a job. While there, he visited his uncle, who was recuperating in the hospital and was sharing a room with an ABC executive. Iger's uncle asked The ABC exec if he could help his nephew get an interview and the executive set up an appointment for Iger to meet with a member of his staff. Iger was interviewed for an open position as a studio supervisor and got the job. He started on July 1, 1974, and after years of outstanding work, he is the Chairman of the Walt Disney Company, ABC's parent company.

One of the first shows Iger worked on was Frank Sinatra: the Main Event, a live concert telecast on ABC. It was produced by Roone Arledge, who was then the president of ABC Sports, and since it was broadcast live, Arledge used members of the ABC Sports' staff to telecast the Sinatra show. Iger met and worked with the ABC Sports staff and a few months later they hired him. He spent 13 years at ABC Sports, rising to the position of Vice President of Programming. Igar says that he never would have gotten that job if he hadn't been assigned to the Frank Sinatra concert and worked with the ABC Sports' staff.

Don't be like the person who stands before a counter jam packed with assorted pastries, wags his/her finger and says, "I want that." Don't make your contacts guess; don't waste their time. Tell them exactly what you want; be specific! Even close friends, who truly want to help, will lose patience if you are not clear and specific … after all, they're not mind readers.

Consider the example Larry Benet, co-founder of SANG offered in our interview. "I think you become who you surround yourself with and everyone says their network equals their net worth. What I would suggest strongly to people is being more strategic. I'll give you a perfect example, as I'm fairly new out here living in Los Angeles. Let's just say I wanted to get to know some local realtors. Well, there is a ton of realtors that I could probably get to know.

"Now, I happen to notice that there is one real estate agent, for example, who happens to be on this *Real Housewives of Beverly Hills*. He is one of the husbands of one of the wives. He finished #7 in the United States for all real estate sales for an agent and I think he is on track to do $600 or $700 million. Now, here is the thing. I do not even know the guy, but I could easily reach out to him and say, 'Hey, I'd like to get to know you for no other reason than I might want to refer you business in the future. Can we have a 15-minute cup of coffee?'

Here is the point. He is incredibly knowledgeable and very influential in what he does, so one of the things that I've been able to do over time is surround myself with a lot of world class experts so I could tap into those experts for a whole host of reasons."

When you fail to request precisely what you seek:

- You risk getting less than you want
- Lack of clarity opens the door for misunderstandings
- If your request is misunderstood, you will probably be disappointed with the results and
- You will still be obligated to return you contact's favor.

To reduce the possibility of misunderstandings, explain what you want in easily understandable language. In order to help you, the people who you approach will often have to contact someone else. When you explain you needs in clear, unmistakable terms, your contacts will instantly know what you want, remember what you requested and be in a better position to accurately communicate it to others.

Never assume that network members, no mater how bright or accomplished they may seem or how many degrees they hold, understand buzzwords, technical language, words of art or occupational-specific terminology. Keep it clear and simple. Remember, your objective is to clearly communicate, not to confuse or try to impress.

Confusion

We all go through times when we are unsure or vague about our what we want. It happens to everyone. Usually, it occurs when our ideas have not crystallized and we have not fully researched or thought them through. Frequently, we only know that we need a job, would like to attend college or find a place to live, but we haven't settled on a specific career, particular colleges or acceptable neighborhoods. In many cases, we have not yet identified the steps we should take to reach our goal. We may know that we need help, but we are not sure what kind of help we need nor who can help us.

At this point, many quit; they make no attempt to move forward. Others tend to take some action, to play it by ear without a plan. They usually put the cart before the horse because they delude themselves into thinking that they will recognize the "right thing" when they see it, which unfortunately isn't always true. It's hard to see the "right thing" when you don't know what you're looking for.

In networking, your requests must be specific.

- First, specific requests enable you to communicate more clearly. When targets quickly understand your request, they are more likely to deliver what you need or promptly refer you to others who can. When you are uncertain, your targets will also be uncertain and less able to deliver what you want. When well-meaning contacts are forced to guess what, it's usually a disaster. Most of the time, confused contacts do not provide any real help, their valuable time is wasted and they will be reluctant to extend themselves for you in the future.

- Second, networking works best when you request help from targets who are experts and well connected in specific fields. If you haven't identified your purpose, how can you identify the best targets? When contacts wander outside their area or expertise, they generally are less successful.

If you are unclear about what you want, figure it out before you go any further. Use the space below to compile a list that will help you define your purpose. List below:

1. Your ideal: the best possible job, college, home, etc. that you could desire
2. The factors that make it your ideal. List the factors in order of their importance. For example, if you got that design job, you could work from home, help out with the kids and save some child care costs.
3. Your bottom line, the least that you would be willing to accept

YOUR IDEAL	THE FACTORS	BOTTOM LINE

Examine your list to determine whether your wishes are realistic. If they are unrealistic, determine what you could do to make them viable. Could they be attainable if you had more training, experience or time? Are the shortcomings things that you could or want to overcome? Do you have better alternatives? Is it worth it to you?

Also ask whether the factors that shaped your ideals are otherwise attainable. If so, decide whether it would be easier, wiser or more rewarding to pursue those options. In you analysis, you may find that certain factors are more important to you than your ideal. In that case, it may be wiser to adjust your ideal.

If, after completing this exercise, you can't identify your purpose, seek guidance. We've all been lost, confused or just stuck in ruts. Most of the time, a good talk or two with close friends, family members, mentors and business associates will help you work it through. But sometimes, the ruts are just too deep. In that event, consider contacting professionals who are in the business of providing expert guidance and advice. Consider their fees a sound investment in your future.

Compelling vision

Business success coach and author Caterina Rando takes the concept of identifying your purpose an additional step further. She teaches that to succeed, you must have a compelling vision. Rando believes that your compelling vision must be so powerful that it rouses you out of bed in the morning and propels you through the day.

According to Rando, you must see and feel your vision. She recommends picturing yourself at the point when you have achieved your objective. For example, close your eyes and actually see the Mayor dedicating your sculpture in the park, waiters serving your apple strudel at the Four Seasons Restaurant, crossing home plate in the World Series at Fenway Park, accepting flowers at the Metropolitan Opera or exchanging vows with the man/woman of your dreams on a tropical South Seas island. See it in full color on a huge Imax screen, smell the aromas and hear all the sounds. Put yourself in the picture.

To be achievable, your compelling vision must have a powerful emotional component. In other words, you must feel it with passion, hunger or need. Strong emotions are the fuel that power and sustain your quests; they underlie the commitment that drives you to attain your dream. To achieve success, your desire to fulfill your vision must be stronger and more alluring than the obstacles you will face in trying to achieve it. And you <u>will</u> encounter obstacles, count on them.

Identifying people

Before you begin to network:

- Identify individuals you want to meet
- Research your targets
- Have a marketable expertise

Justin Spizman, Award Winning and Best-Selling Author and Rick's go-to Ghostwriter said, "In my career as a writer, I have always focused efforts on targeting specific people who I felt could use help writing a book. Maybe they needed to build a platform, or tell a story, or transition into a new career. Regardless, I knew we could collaborate together. I would search my network to find a colleague who could connect me with the potential client. It started small, but through identifying individuals, researching their needs, and marketing my expertise, I have built a client base that consists of well-known athletes, entrepreneurs, professional coaches, CEO's and celebrities. Through working with Rick, I have been connected to an amazing network with a genuine need for a Ghostwriter which has helped to grow my business and work on some pretty exciting projects."

When selecting potential targets, think first in terms of categories. Do you want to connect with a surgeon who specializes in repairing cardiac valves, a moving company that can safely transport valuable art works across the country or an automobile mechanic who can expertly repair vintage Mustang convertibles?

After you've identified your category, you may discover that you don't know people who can help you reach your objective. Generally, the best approach is research. Books, articles, Web sites and your network members can usually give you names of and information about your potential targets. In your research, learn as much as possible about your potential targets because the information you acquire could be the basis for making connections.

Targets that you identify may be beyond your reach. Trying to contact them directly is usually impossible so investigate whether you can reach them through intermediaries.

NETWORKING NUGGET

When Dennis Crow of Pierce & Crow, a leading high technology executive search firm, began his business, he had a strong background in high tech operations, but no executive search experience. So he called upon social friends and business contacts including those who had invested in his former business. Crow told them about his new business, his plans and asked if they would introduce him to key people in their businesses.

One contact, a partner in Silicone Valley's most powerful venture capital firm, invited Crow to his office where they discussed Crow's plans and prospects. At Crow's request, the venture capitalist agreed to send a letter introducing Crow to his business buddies. Crow drafted a letter, which his contact edited, put on his letterhead and sent to 44 of the who's who of the venture capital community.

Within six weeks, Crow had 44 appointments. Not only did he meet 44 top high tech executives, but virtually all of them had the venture capitalist's letter sitting prominently on their desks. Although it took time and hard work to get their business, Crow credits the letter for jump starting his business and getting it launched.

Turn to your network to make the connections. Jeff Kahn, Chief Strategic Officer of AudioCodes, suggests using line extensions to map your route. If you want to get to Dr. X, make a list of all of the information you've learned about him through your research: where he works, where he lives, his background, his affiliations and his interests. Then draw a line from Dr. X through your network contacts until you find connections.

- Examine you network membership list and identify who might lead you to your target.
- Ask network members if they know Dr. X, if they have contacts who can perform delicate cardiac valve surgery or know of people who have suffered from heart valve problems. If so, contact them.
- Spread the word widely. Let everyone in your network know your objective and your target.
- Ask your network members if they have contacts who work in health care and insurance and, if so, get in touch with their contacts.

Ask your contacts if they know, or know of, each recommended doctor and/or his/her patients. If they do, ask about their experience. Also ask:

Were they happy with the doctor's work?
Were there problems?
What did they like or dislike?
Would they use that doctor again?

If they don't personally know about the doctor, ask if they know others who do and if you can use their names to contact them.

Also check with the doctors' hospitals, local medical associations, your insurance agent and even your lawyer.

As we previously explained, to play in the networking league, you must be prepared to give something in exchange for each contact's help. In chapter two, we asked you to inventory your personal assets. We requested that you list what you could provide to reciprocate for your target's help. Review that list and if you haven't completed it, please do so now before continuing further.

Networking events

When you attend networking events, your purpose must be clear. In most cases, it's to get exposure or make contacts for business, nonprofit, philanthropic, social or family reasons or simply to escape. When you go to a Chamber of Commerce mixer, Book Expo or a Sierra Club meeting, you're generally hoping to meet or hang around people who attend these events. Similarly, when you go to a café that caters to musicians, you want to meet or spend time with musicians or music lovers.

David Hancock, Chief Evangelist for the Entrepreneur Author and Founder and CEO of Morgan James Publishing, told us, "When I attend networking events, I am focused on the goal. I know that balance does not come easily. To succeed, I must remain focused on my journey, seeing the future clearly while concentrating on the present. I am aware that the minutia of life and business can distract me, so I do what is necessary to make those distractions only momentary."

Before attending networking events such as conventions, conferences, association meetings and mixers, ask yourself:

- Why you are going?
- Who will be there?
- Who you hope to meet?
- What do you know about them?
- What you hope to get from them?
- What is the best way to approach them?
- How you can reciprocate?

When you answer these questions, conduct more research to be better prepared. Use the Internet, it's a mother load of terrific information that is easy to access. Preparation will improve your focus and your prospects of making the event more productive.

Other places and events

When you go to that café that caters to musicians, or to the ballet, the aquarium, or a PTA meeting, networking is seldom your primary motivation. However, networking opportunities can always arise at nonnetworking events. Since the best contacts can be made in the unlikeliest, most unplanned-for situations, you must be alert to all networking opportunities and be prepared to react. You also must take pains to act appropriately.

NETWORKING NUGGET

Food stylist George DoLese was biding time in a long line at a New York City pastry shop the man behind him started talking to him. Initially, he complained about the long wait, but both he and LoLese agreed that he pastries were worth it. The conversation then moved on to pastries and food in general. As DoLese reached the counter, the man handed DoLese his business card and asked him to call. He was the executive chef at a restaurant owned by Donald Trump and had an opening that he thought would be ideal for DoLese. DoLese called, got the job and an amazing experience working for Trump.

Even the most casual meeting can be an interview or an opportunity. In the time they waited together, DoLese was able to convey his expertise and this landed him a terrific job. He was prepared and when the opportunity presented itself, even in the most unexpected place, he was able to capitalize on it.

We've all heard millions of similar stories; how someone profited from being at the right spot at the right time. However, these bonanzas aren't simply the product of dumb luck. True, they may have been fortunate to be where they were, but they also had the ability to provide a good impression and to make the best of the opportunity.

However, reacting to perceived opportunities in nonnetworking situations can be tricky. Although it might be tempting to jump on opportunities that present themselves during school board meetings, it may not be worth the risk of offending others in attendance. Inappropriate networking can be disruptive and impolite. It can sully your reputation and alienate people who could help you somewhere down the line.

So be alert to networking opportunities at nonnetworking situations, but pursue possible contacts only if it feels 100 percent appropriate. Don't make a move if you have the slightest doubt. Usually, it's simply a matter of timing and since networking is not the primary reason for your presence, the best approach is to wait for a break or until the main business has concluded to pursue your quarry. Then make contact, exchange business cards or contact information and arrange to call or meet at a later date. If making contact might be at all awkward, uncomfortable or disruptive, save it for a more appropriate time.

Often the best networking tactic is to concentrate on the situation at hand rather than attempting to make network contacts. By focusing on the business on hand, you can demonstrate your abilities and dedication to the cause. As a result, others will usually be impressed and want to get to know you better. So concentrate on your purpose in being present and contribute. Build your reputation and the contacts will follow. Do good by doing good.

Prioritize

Select your targets precisely and limit the number of targets you pursue. Instead of trying to saturate large groups, initially concentrate on reaching a few key people who can provide concrete help. Often, when you try to cover everything, you end up handling little well.

Choose a few realistic targets and focus in on them. Identify potential targets and research them thoroughly. Find out everything about them and become expert on their strong points, passions, weaknesses, interests, aversions, hobbies, families, background, habits, histories and connections. See how they link with your strong points, passions, weaknesses, interests, aversions, hobbies, families, background, habits, histories and connections. What you learn through your research will give you insights on how to approach them and how to build and maintain a rewarding relationship when you've connected.

NETWORKING NUGGET

Writer, speaker and trainer, Dave Sherman, gave us a great example why he is called "The Networking Guy." A good friend of Dave's was laid off from her job of 8 years and needed to quickly find another job. She contacted Dave who first identified what she was looking for and then sent an email to his 2,600 member network requesting their help in finding a job for his friend.

In less than 24 hours, Dave received well over 200 emails and at least 25 telephone calls with offers to help his friend. From the responses, he learned about over 80 job openings, many of which were good jobs with great companies. In less a week, Dave's friend landed a great new job at a bank that offered her better pay and better benefits than her last job. That is the power of networking!

When Dave's friend called Dave, she contacted someone who had the ability to quickly reach over 2,600 people with a single email. If she had not known Dave, it could have taken her forever to reach that many contacts.

Make sure that your targets have the ability to provide what you want. Remember that you have limited time, resources and energy and if you try to cover too much you could squander your valuable assets. When you have too many targets, it's difficult to give each the attention it deserves. When you have too many balls in the air, it takes only one misstep for most of them to fall. Spreading yourself thinly makes it harder to maintain control. It reduces the likelihood of success and leads to your becoming discouraged. So target precisely because you don't want to waste your precious time pursuing the wrong people or attending irrelevant meetings.

Be realistic. Don't shoot for the brightest stars unless you have a realistic chance and solid plan for reaching them. Even then, examine the feasibility of approaching every target cautiously.

Powerful people surround themselves with multiple layers of protections that are specifically designed to keep the uninvited away. To reach them, you have to circumvent electronic fences, which can be time consuming and frustrating … like sitting forever on hold and being treated coldly. And when you reach celebrity targets, they may not deliver. So don't waste your time trying to go where you're not wanted. If you have a strong lead, pursue it, but expect resistance. When you feel strong resistance, politely say "Thanks," move away and focus your efforts on Target Number 2.

Connect the links. Review your network roster and find connections on which to build. Link your connections like a set of steps that will lift you to higher floors. Start with small steps; build and be patient. Prepare for a slow, steady ascent. Don't rush.

Carefully select targets who know you, who you can reach and who can deliver what you need. Start with those who will be happy to help you. Although your close contacts may not be able to deliver as much as celebrated authorities, they are more likely to actually provide what they promise. So start with them and build steadily.

As you grow and make new contacts, build upon them at each stage. Concentrate on developing a reputation for quality, expertise and honesty; become well respected and well known; then people in power will approach you. Move slowly, incrementally and steadily.

Narrowing in

Selecting networking targets is always risky. People and businesses are often not what they seem. Even after the most detailed, probing examinations, certain information never comes to light. Many ingredients are involved in matchmaking. Some of them are hard to measure and others are intangibles or personality based.

Although there is not fool-proof formula for choosing targets, the following questions could eliminate some of the risk:

- Does your target provide products or services that could affect you or your business?
- If so, how?
- Who are your target's customers?
- How do your target's customers fit or relate to your customers?
- How do your customers and you target's customers overlap?
- What geographical area does your target's products or service cover?
- Who are your target's competitors?

- How can you help your target?
- How can your target help you?

Don't be blinded by titles or purported accomplishments. Titleholders may just be flunkies and lack the clout to deliver what you need. Often, those who received credit may not be the ones who actually did the work.

Shoot for the top

Aim for the best that is within your reach. Start locally, identify who you know and determine how they can get you to the top. Plan an incremental approach. Get to know neighborhood association members and then move up to your supervisor, alderman, town councilors, mayor, state representatives, governor, US senators all the way to the White House. All the while, keep learning, building your knowledge base so that when it's combined with your contact base, you will be more desirable.

Occasions will arise when you must have the best. For example, when health is concerned. Instead of settling for any surgeon who repairs heart valves, find the best surgeon for such repairs. Usually, the referral process begins with the cardiologist, who diagnosed the faulty valve. He/she will give you several names. Then it's time to turn to your network. Immediately, get the word out and spread it widely. Call network members who are in health related fields and tell them, "I'm trying to find the best surgeon who specializes in repairing cardiac valves." Ask if they know the surgeons that the cardiologist suggested or have heard of them. If your inquiries are unsuccessful, broaden the search to other members of your network. Often, they will give you the names of others who might help.

Go national

Many local networking organizations are branches or chapters of national organizations. Become active with local groups that have state and national organizations. Start locally and then expand to the state, national and international levels.

When you join a group, attend regularly. To make meaningful contacts, you have to go to more than one or two meetings. Become a recognized presence. Volunteer for committees to demonstrate your abilities. Organization members come and go and groups, on all levels, are always searching for fresh, new talent to fill empty slots. Making a name for yourself on the local level is a wonderful stepping stone to nationwide prominence. And it works visa versa.

Jill is active in the San Francisco chapter of eWomenNetwork. A few years ago, the National Speakers Association booked her to speak in Houston. As soon as she had that booking, Jill called the eWomanNetwork Chapter in Houston and ask it they need a speaker at the time she would be in Houston. The Houston chapter them booked Jill to speak. Even if the Houston Chapter hadn't asked her to speak, Jill being such a dynamic networker would have attended the local chapter meeting or lunch to meet and network with Houston chapter members.

Before you travel to another market, investigate whether the organizations you belong to have branches in the cities you plan to visit. If so, check if they will be holding events at that time that you can attend to expand your network contacts.

★☆★ Action steps ★☆★

---

1. State your purpose, identify exactly why you want to network.

---

2. Describe in full, graphic detail your compelling vision.

_____

_____

_____

3. List four ways that you can research your targets.

_____

_____

_____

4. Write down three ways that you can inoffensively network at nonnetworking events.

_____

_____

_____

CHAPTER 5

POSITION YOURSELF

"Network everywhere and with everyone. Don't wait for a special occasion to enjoy the benefits of networking. You never know where you will make a connection that can change your life."
—**Melissa Wahl**, Vice President Of Development, Womens Presidents' Organization

This chapter will cover:
- ❏ *Become an expert*
- ❏ *Declare your expertise*
- ❏ *Beyond your level*
- ❏ *Get yourself there*
- ❏ *Seminars and Workshops*
- ❏ *Get published*
- ❏ *Get creative*

Networks are built around the exchange of information and networking is information intensive. To be both successful and sustaining, networks must constantly receive an influx of new and relevant information; information that network members can take, analyze and then parcel out to their network partners who then can make the best use of it.

To efficiently utilize the stream of networking information requires knowledge, expert knowledge. First, it requires the knowledge to understand the full implications of the information received and what it means. Second, it requires knowledge about the members of your network, their needs, capabilities and capacities. With this knowledge, members who receive information can then analyze it, determine who can best use it and allocate it to those network partners who can benefit from it.

So, to build and maintain a successful network, you must be an expert. The more knowledgeable you become, the more desirable you will be to potential network partners. Your pretty face, clever wit and winning personality may initially get you noticed, but you will fade as fast as last month's news if you don't have an expertise that others desire.

By becoming an expert, you will make yourself more attractive to those who can give you the greatest help—the in crowd, the movers and shakers, the decision makers and the power brokers. Those at the top, the people with influence, want to associate with the best. They want to do business and socialize with them, and so should you. The surest route for reaching the top is by becoming an expert in your field.

Your expertise is the exchange that you give back to your network partners in return for their help, it's your ticket to the dance. Being an expert simply means that you know what you're doing. It doesn't necessarily mean that you're the world's most recognized authority, although you may be. It also doesn't mean that you know absolutely everything about your field ... no one does!

When you're acknowledged to be an expert, people want to hear what you have to say. Invitations to participate in meetings, panel discussions, workshops and conferences pour in. You will be asked to write about your expertise, enter your work in competitions and contribute your efforts for charitable causes. These opportunities will give you great exposure, terrific PR, extend your influence and introduce to community and industry leaders. In addition, you will be coveted as a speaker, teacher and competition judge, which will introduce you to bright new talents, who will extend the demographic of your network to a younger generation.

You probably are expert in more areas than you realize. If you operate a business, you're probably an expert in your field. You're also probably an expert in activities in which you spend lots of time at such as being a single mother, making ravioli, growing orchids, throwing pots, knitting sweaters, operating a home-based office, coaching a Pee Wee League team or skiing. In addition, you're an expert in intangible areas including being well organized, fair minded, efficient, reliable, punctual, reasonable, wise, understanding, considerate and courageous.

> Your expertise enhances your value to your network. Each area of expertise adds special flavors that make your contributions to the network desirable and unique; they give your contributions added worth. For example, your ability to operate a home-based office may prove invaluable to a network member who just left a large corporate job to start a new business in his/her garage; your even handedness and good judgment may help resolve troubling differences within your networking group.

Expertise is always with you. If you were awakened in the middle of the night and cross examined about your area of interest, despite being groggy, despite being extremely cross, you could snap off all the right answer right there on the spot. When networking opportunities arise, you possess the information, you have the expert knowledge that you can use, but you must be prepared to showcase it.

Be alert to opportunities to demonstrate your expertise and be prepared to capitalize on them. Don't abruptly or inappropriately force your expertise on listeners, but be patient. Wait for appropriate openings when what you have to say will be relevant and further the conversation. Learn to bide your time and listen to what others are saying. Then, when and if opportunity knocks, move fast because it may not come again.

NETWORKING NUGGET

Whenever possible, Ken Browning, a prominent Beverly Hills entertainment attorney, always tries to help his clients by introducing them to his extensive contacts. Browning represented a well-known celebrity who was featured in an infomercial for a major cosmetics company. While representing her, he developed a relationship with a management executive for the cosmetics company, who subsequently asked Browning to represent the company in a number of matters. Several years later, hair stylist Nick Chavez asked Browning to become his partner in developing a line of hair care products. Browning connected Chavez with the cosmetics company, which showed great interest in his line, but the company ultimately decided to go in a different direction.

A few years later, the cosmetics executive left the company to become the director of beauty at a cable-shopping network. In a conversation with her, Browning inquired whether she would be interested in selling Chavez's product line through her network. As a result, Perfect Plus, the Browning/Chavez company, went on the network, where it sold out its initial offering in record time and became the network's best selling hair care line.

The success of Perfect Plus, also boosted Browning's law practice by attracting a steady stream of companies that sell their products via infomercials and home shopping outlets and the television exposure increased Chavez's salon clientele.

In your quest for knowledge, learn as much as you possibly can about your new contacts and your network partners. When you meet people, find out as much about them as you can, become an expert on them. Discover what they do, what they like, what they dislike and what they need. Identify their interests them and get information about their families and backgrounds.

Discretely ask them about themselves, get them talking. Also ask your network partners about them.

> Note when a contact mentions that she is involved in boating or wants to get her kids into a drama camp. Then train yourself to look for published items about those interests and send them to her with a brief note, "Thought this might interest you." Use your knowledge about your contacts to connect them with business contacts who could help them.

Finding leads for network partners is an essential part of networking. In order to hook your partners up with the best potential matches, requires you to know what they want and need.

- Question your network partners about their interests
- Visit their places of business
- Discover what they want,
- Find out what they need and
- Ask how you can help.

Learning about your network partners also has the secondary benefits of broadening your knowledge, exposing you to and teaching you about new areas. These new areas could help you in the future and send you in directions that you would be impossible to presently imagine.

In Chapter 2, we asked you to inventory your personal assets. Now, review that list and prioritize your personal assets according to what you consider your greatest strengths. In reviewing the list, pinpoint the contributions you can provide to individual members of your network and how they would support their goals. In your review, also ask how you can adjust what you can contribute to suit particular situations or enhance its value and increase its demand.

Declare your expertise

Tell others about your expertise and why it's so special. Find ways to promote yourself by writing articles; giving talks; giving demonstrations; starting Web sites, joining groups and participating in conferences, workshops and discussions. Volunteer your service to build your reputation and impress people who may be in a position to help you.

Write or talk about tasks that you've performed a thousand times: how to write a press release, how to barbeque fish or how to care for tropical fish. Teach others, step by step, how to do it.

- Write articles. Prepare two written versions: one 1,500 words and the other 800 words. Be ready to recite them on short notice
- Always have copies of both articles on hand to distribute
- Keep your articles simple and don't try to state everything you know. Cover no more than seven points, no less than three
- Make your articles practical, not theoretical: How to Write A Movie Review, Five Easy Steps to Weight Loss or How to Make Seamless Welds That Last.

Send your articles to publications, organizations, Web sites in your field or related fields and to your network. Follow up with e-mails or phone calls. Offer yourself as an expert speaker. Recite your article aloud as speeches. Prepare visual aids such as slides, illustrations and charts. Practice them on your family and friends.

At the end of articles, include your bio and state who you are, what you do, how you can be reached and your message. Prepare a more extensive bio that can be distributed during your speaking engagements.

Testimonials

Reap greater rewards from your accomplishments by obtaining testimonials and endorsements. Business expert Mitch Axelrod maintains that, "Word of mouth is still your best advertising. Most people don't take full advantage of the word of mouth benefits they can get from their clients. The most powerful marketing tool is not what you say, but what others say about you. So get testimonials and endorsements from your customers and clients. People pay attention to them. They are the highest, most specific and deepest praise you can get."

- Ask each of your clients/customers for a letter of praise.
- Ask them to state how great your work was and how much they enjoyed working with you. You'll be surprised how highly they praise you and how well they express it.
- Ask for endorsements as soon as the projects are complete
- Ask your clients/customers to write your testimonials on their stationary and tell them to hold them to two or three paragraphs
- Ask each client/customer to give call or give you the names of three friends or associates who may be interested in you product or services. Ask if you can use their name, and better yet, if they would be willing to call or write their friends recommending you or introduce you to them in person
- Accumulate endorsements, build your own personal collection; they're invaluable for getting business
- Explain to clients/customers that you plan to post the testimonials on your newsletter, Web sight and promotional materials
- Point out to your clients/customers how their testimonials could help them by increasing their visibility
- If clients hesitate, offer to prepare drafts for their editing and approval
- Update Web sites regularly to add recent testimonials and to remove those that are dated. However, run a few old testimonials because they show that you have a long track record of customer satisfaction
- Carry copies of your testimonials and endorsements whenever you might have a chance to get new business.

Letters to the editor

Show your expertise in letters to editors and by posting comments in Web chat rooms. If you want to get involved in your community, letters to editors will make you name, positions and expertise know. Well-reasoned articles and comments will also help you build a following, promote your name recognition and build your stature and extend your network.

People like to deal with the best. It builds their confidence because they believe it improves their chances for success. Being associated with the best is prestigious and gives your contacts something to crow about. Our world is star struck and celebrity driven. How many times have you heard friends say, "Guess, who I just saw?" And then they proudly reel off the name of some celebrity who they passed on the street. Those who are considered the best or stars in their fields can charge more so and there is greater demand for their products and services.

Beyond your level

All too frequently, the people we want to meet, those who could quickly catapult us into the upper galaxies, are beyond our reach. Not only don't we know them, but we don't know anyone else who can reach them. Calling them blindly without a warm introduction is futile and email seldom works. Occasionally, an email will slip through, but it's a long, long shot.

To reach the unreachable, you must cultivate the relationship, and even that may not work. The best plan, according to professional speaker and marketing consultant Ken Glickman, is sending personal letters. The chances of succeeding still remain slim, but one of your letters could touch a responsive chord and yield substantial rewards.

Glickman suggests writing a personal letter that states, "I've followed your career (read your book/article, saw your interview) and respect what you are doing. I wonder there are any books that you could recommend to me that had a major influence on your life or career." Most powerful people won't respond, but some just might.

If any of the people you write do respond, read the book or books they recommend and when you've finished it, send a brief note saying, "I read the book and found it very useful. Thank you very much." Keep it brief. Just say thanks and nothing more. Let it go at that and move on.

If, thereafter, your career advances … you get recognition, an award, a better job, a promotion or a good raise … then send another note saying, "I just wanted you to know that I was promoted or did _____ and want to thank you. I attribute a great part of my success to _____, the book you recommended." You can leave it at that or ask him/her to recommend another book.

This technique keeps you in touch, lets your contact know that you're doing well and helps you build a relationship that could turn into a deeper, mentoring relationship. At the same time, it builds name recognition and creates a favorable impression. If, somewhere along the line, you meet you will have established a solid basis on which to further the relationship.

Get yourself there

Put your self in places and positions where the magic can occur. As Woody Allen said, "Showing up is 80 percent of life."

"Schedule yourself to be in the right places where you can meet the targets you seek," Jeff Kahn, the Chief Strategic Officer at AudioCodes, advises. "I've met at least a third of the people who became my good friends or people who became my business customers in the first class airline lounges or in business class plane seats. Choose the gym where you work out not just because of its equipment, but also factor in the people who you will be there that you interact with."

Kahn, who is in public relations, works out in a gym frequented by celebrities and policy makers. "The interactions at the gym forge bonds that are stronger than those created at terse business meetings because they're based on shared experienced. They go beyond just transactional or business dealings. Every choice you make ... where you work out, where you eat lunch ... creates opportunities. If you have an idea where you want to go in life, then those choices will create better opportunities for you," Kahn stressed.

Get out of the office or the house and expose yourself to people and experiences that can move you in new and exciting directions. Relinquish some of the control that may keep you languishing in the same old place, repeating the same task and making the same mistakes. Expose yourself because you never can predict what might happen.

NETWORKING NUGGET

Personal branding expert Karen McCullough had just closed the retail business that she ran for over 20 years to become a speaker. As her new career was starting to pick up, Karen's friend Mary invited her to accompany her to Jazzfest in New Orleans, which was to be held the last weekend of April. Karen agreed and bought a ticket, but a few weeks later, she was asked to speak at a major event. However, the event conflicted with Jazzfest so Karen decided to forego Jazzfest, stay home and worry.

When she called Mary to cancel, Mary reminded Karen that she had worked day and night, weekends and holidays in retail. Karen had blamed retail for her empty life and now it looked like she was repeating the same mistakes. "The first thing you have to do in life," Mary explained, "is show up." So, Karen heeded her advice and agreed to go to New Orleans.

Jazzfest was an absolute blast! Great food, drinks, music, people and fun in the sun. On the final day, Sting was the headliner. Although Karen had never seen him in concert, she fell in love with him that night.

At 6:30, Karen had to leave to catch her flight home. She said goodbye to Mary, waved up at Sting and I sadly left the fairgrounds. The thought of returning to work the next day sent pangs of fear deep into the pit of her stomach; after all that jazz, Karen had a bad case of the Sunday Night Blues.

In line at the airport, Karen spotted a guy in front of her who resembled Sting. As they bent over to pick up their bags, she still wasn't sure if it was Sting. Karen didn't want to ask him if he was Sting, but she really wanted to know. Then it hit her. As his ear passed by her mouth, she started singing, "Roxanne you don't have to do do do da." She didn't know the words. Then he looked up, smiled and softly sang, "Turn on the red light." It really was Sting!

> Sting and Karen walked down the jetway, talking without stop like old friends. He walked her to her gate, said good-bye and began walking away to catch a flight for Los Vegas. As Karen watched him leave, she suddenly heard a voice yell "Sting." It was her voice. As he turned, Karen ran to him, grabbed his face and kissed him.
>
> That's when Karen understood why they call him Sting!

Watch out for comfort, being comfortable can be a trap. It can keep you in bed, in the house and in the same old same old where it's hard to progress. Comfort can stymie growth and keep you treading water. Although we all work to be more comfortable, comfort can be a trap. So, break old habits, break the mold, take chance, do something daring and try something new.

Seminars and workshops

Seminars and workshops are ideal for increasing your expertise and networking. Attending them can:

- Polish your skills
- Bring you up to speed on industry developments
- Introduce you to new areas
- Introduce you to new people
- Put you in contact with authorities and
- Help build your network.

Seminars are great for networking because everyone is in the same industry or has the same basic interests. When you have common interests, networking becomes far easier and more natural. Introductions and explanations can be shorter or even eliminated because the joint experience of learning, asking and problem solving in your own field takes over and creates a bond.

At seminars, you can meet, learn from and forge relationships with renowned experts and your peers. As a student you can feel a sense of camaraderie and sharing with your peers that enables you to make new friends, friends who can become network members. Often you new friends will be from different areas, which can extend your reach and help you to grow.

If the benefits of attending seminars and workshops are good, the rewards from leading or teaching them are stratospheric. Leading or teaching seminars and workshops helps you network by increasing your visibility, reputation and stature. It positions you as an important and respected authority as well as a leader in your field. It makes you the subject of more attention, and if you're good, of more respect. As an acknowledged authority, you can extend your influence so that you can meet and network with others on or above your plane, the authorities at the top of your field.

When you lead seminars and workshops, you get to demonstrate your expertise to attendees who are eager to hear you what you have to say. As a leader, you can exchange ideas and help solve problems with the top minds and the most successful players in your field.

Create your own

Appearing at seminars is so desirable that the competition between speakers is brutal. If you're not in demand as a speaker, volunteer to help at other events. It will give you exposure to important, powerful people, position you as an insider and teach you how to operate workshops, seminars and other events.

After apprenticing for a while, you may be ready to create, organize or lead your own seminar. Running your own seminar can be extremely lucrative and let you make invaluable contacts. It will also, enable you test whether you enjoy operating seminars and if you do it well.

Start small, learn on the job and work your way up. Establish a track record for excellence. Starting small also limits your financial risk. Identify topics that can draw large audiences. If you're a professional ballet dancer, run a seminar to show mothers of aspiring dancers what your career entails; if you're a realtor, teach people how to buy houses and secure mortgages and if you're a psychologist, teach stress reduction techniques. Give practical, hands-on, how-to instructions so attendees return home with tangible benefits.

In the beginning, don't charge, offer free seminars or just cover your costs. Consider what you learn from the experience as ample compensation. Plus, you will be building a following because those who enjoy the event, will return, be your supporters and join your network.

Try to convince a local charity, religious, civic or social group to allow you to use their facility in exchange for a modest contribution and/or publicity. If that fails, rent a room.

To promote your seminar, call upon your network. Print posters and fliers and have your network members help you place them in high traffic areas such as schools, universities, community centers, libraries and businesses in or related to your field. Send announcements to local radio stations and related Web sites. Get names from your network, name lists and local organizations. Send post cards or fliers announcing the event. Promote your seminar on the Web at sites. Send e-mails to you network and ask them to send it to their networks.

WARNING: Running seminars can be difficult, demanding work so instead of trying to operate your own, consider offering your services as a lecturer to organizations that sponsor such events. Unless you've got a big reputation, don't even think of starting at the top. Instead, begin by volunteering your services to local organizations and then, as you gain skill and recognition, moving to bigger, more prestigious events.

Service clubs: To get experience, start with local service clubs. They are perfect venues for making and learning from mistakes. Local service clubs are equivalent to comedy clubs where comics, both experienced and novice, go to polish their material and try out new routines. Give yourself the freedom to mistakes and learn from them.

Volunteer to speak at events sponsored by the Elks Club, the Rotary Club, the Veterans of Foreign Wars, the Chamber of Commerce, Women in Business, religious, business, civic groups, etc. Don't ask to be paid, chalk it up to your education. Consider these opportunities to perfect your presentation, build your reputation and meet potential customers/clients, contacts and the media.

WARNING: Certain local organizations appeal mainly to retirees or to a demographic that might not interest you. While events sponsored by these groups may provide opportunities to sharpen your presentation, they may not be the right places for you to network. So when you book engagements, <u>factor in the audience profile</u>.

Get experience, build a reputation and network by teaching a workshop or even a course for local educational institutions such as community colleges or adult education programs. Participate in online conferences. Approach businesses that provide adult education and career-development courses.

<u>Conferences and conventions</u>: With the exception of Oprah, the Today Show, , Larry King or your own infomercial, conferences and conventions are the top. Speaking at major conferences puts you at the pinnacle of your industry provides unlimited networking opportunities. Speakers and instructors usually receive an honorarium and their travel/lodging expenses are paid.

At conferences and conventions, the presentations are ostensibly about learning. In reality; however, they're equally about networking, socializing and fellowship. People attend as much to make contacts as to learn.

If you get the chance to speak at a conference or convention, become a performer. Spice up your presentations with humor, anecdotes and real-life stories. Be newsy. Everyone loves inside scoops about people, companies and gossip in their business. Update the latest industry developments and make yourself available to those in attendance. Focus on a few hot topics that people in your industry should learn and cover them expertly. Encourage questions from the audience. Make yourself available after you've completed your presentation. Run off copies of news developments, articles, examples, reading lists and abstracts of presentations so that attendees feel that they're getting value. Provide a list of the names and contact information for who signed up for your sessions.

Popular speakers and authors, such as *Chicken Soup for the Soul* co-author Mark Victor Hansen, command handsome fees to lead seminars and address conferences. However, they routinely make even more selling a wide assortment of materials during their appearances. For example, they sell books, audiotapes, videotapes, workbooks, calendars and novelty items from the back of the room. They also get names for list that they can sell.

Promoters estimate that 20 to 25 percent of those who attend presentations at conferences and convention buy speakers' goods. And, the top attractions exceed those amounts. Veteran speakers frequently offer discounted packages of their materials. They might package three or four items that usually sell for $250 for half that price. To encourage sales, they'll autograph their wares, chat with attendees, pose for photographs and dance with you wife. Audiences, inspired by rousing speakers, gobble up goods that will remind them of, or supplement, the experience ... especially when the speaker has personally autographed them.

Get published

To increase your credibility, your profile and your attractiveness to networkers, get publish. Being a published author gives you more than credibility, it gives you the elevated status of being an authority. Authoring a book, and to a lesser degree articles, gives you recognition as an expert.

A book is a powerful networking tool because:

- Authors are respected and sought after.
- Giving potential network member or target can tip the scales in your favor. It creates instant good will and writing a personalized message will thaw the most glacial and convert total strangers into grateful, loyal, long-standing devotees.
- Once your book is published, your status as an expert becomes permanent, it can never be taken away. You're listed in the Library of Congress, in the Copyright Office and with amazon.com. The local media competes to interview you, you get cool invitations and attract conference groupies. Being a published author is exciting and satisfying . . . it's fame lasts far more than 15 minutes!
- The exhilaration of authorship is addictive. Once published, virtually all authors want to repeat the experience. Subsequent books reinforce their status and further their careers. Public admiration and respect is intoxicating.
- Books don't have to be lengthy Frankly, most people never read them so they don't know whether your book is long or short, good or bad or in English or Mandarin. However, when they learn you've written a book, they're invariably impressed and usually try to get to know you.

- Most authors don't make money from selling their books, but their books help propel their careers. And, you never know, there's always a chance that your book will make the bestseller list, you'll appear on Jay and Dave and hit the jackpot!

Get creative

Find unusual ways to distinguish yourself and to stand out from the crowd. Use inventive, creative approaches to show targets and potential network partners that you're someone with flair, vision, imagination and a great sense of humor. Think boldly and give people a laugh. Everyone loves a good laugh; it lowers their guard and makes them more receptive.

Design you business cards, brochures, literature and Web site to attract positive attention. Examine the profile of the targets you want to reach and determine the looks and approaches they like. Identify the styles that are standard for your groups. Then build on their standards, but then play with them, take them a few steps further and push the envelope.

Test the waters before going public. Bounce your ideas off your friends and network partners. Check their reactions and heed their feedback. It's easy to go overboard, to lose your compass and get lost in playfulness. Always keep in mind that your objective is to attract favorable attention, not to come off as a fool or a clown.

NETWORKING NUGGET

Author Randy Peyser was growing desperate. Her landlords had just informed her that they were giving the great little cottage she had rented for the past six years to their daughter who was about to graduate from college. Finding new housing that would accept Randy and her old Springer spaniel, Cookie, was proving impossible. Since all of the traditional methods of finding housing were not working, Randy decided to get creative. She made a sign that said, "RENTAL NEEDED, INQUIRE WITHIN." She taped the sign across the front of her T-shirt and went to a giant picnic that was attended by several hundred people.

Randy's sign was a big hit at the picnic; it gave everyone a good laugh. A woman approached Randy and said that she had a room in her home to rent. Randy explained that she had a dog, but the woman replied, "Oh, that's not a problem, I love dogs." Randy checked out the room, liked it and moved in. Although she only expected to stay until she found a larger place, which she thought would be a few months at the most, Randy and Cookie lived there happily for nearly two and a half years.

★★★ Action steps ★★★

1. Name three ways that you can declare your expertise.

_____

_____

_____

2. Identify five customers or clients who can give you written testimonials.

_____

_____

_____

3. List three individuals who you admire, but are beyond your reach that you will write letters to.

_____

_____

_____

4. On what subjects could you write articles or book?

_____

_____

_____

CHAPTER 6

YOUR NETWORKING TOOLKIT

*"My networking magic formula is to make contacts
to get contracts and multiply my exposure to source,
serve and motivate everyone I encounter."*
—**Mark Victor Hansen**, Best Selling Author

This chapter will cover:
- ❏ *Sound bites*
- ❏ *Writing your sound bite*
- ❏ *Delivering your message*
- ❏ *Description of you, your product or service*
- ❏ *Business cards*
- ❏ *Address lists, calendars and writing materials.*

When you call professionals to repair a major appliance in your home, they bring the right tools to handle the job. Similarly, good networkers are always equipped with the tools that they need to do a great job. The networkers' tool kit consists of:

- A fabulous sound bite
- A great description of you, your product or service
- Business cards
- An address list
- A date book or mobile device calendar
- Writing materials and
- Expertise

Picture yourself entering a room jam that is packed with strangers all talking intently in tight little clusters. As you walk in, you scan the room hoping to spot a familiar face, but there is no one you know, not a single soul. So you head towards the table piled high with snacks trying to look confident and hoping your jitters subside. As you're walking, you try to figure out your next move, but then your eyes make contact with a pleasant looking chap standing to your right. Talking with him are two nicely dressed women. As you draw closer, he turns toward you, sticks out his hand, introduces himself and beckons you to the group. The women smile softly, say hello, state their names and extend their hands. And presto, your smack dab in the middle of a conversation with three total strangers.

After a few opening niceties, one of the women looks you squarely in the eyes and inquires, "What do you do?" Although it's said pleasantly, you can sense her focus, you can tell that she's all business. You realize that she is really asking, "Who are you and why should I spend my valuable time talking with you?"

At that moment,

- Do you have the right answer?
- Do you know exactly what to say?
- Do you have a killer sound bite ready to reel off for just such occasions that can transform a perfect stranger into a network ally?

- Have you practiced that sound bite so that you can flawlessly rattle it off?
- Do you have a great business card?
- Can you give a quick, clear description of what you offer?

Well, you should!

Sound bites

A sound bite is your opening, your introduction, your verbal calling card. It's a succinct, memorable, defining statement that explains *who you are*, *what you do* and *how you can help*. A sound bite is your keynote, so make it good!

In networking, sound bites are essential. We live in a world where few people have time for the full story. Even at networking events that people attend to make contacts, they're always scanning the room, planning their next move and they seldom give you their full attention. When they need information, they want condensed versions, digests, capsules that that take only seconds to deliver, are easy to grasp, lock in their mind and are easy to recall.

It's hard to get people to listen. They're overwhelmed by endless demands. Everyone wants to take their time and energy. Most of the people you want to reach can't spare a moment, they're overbooked and overloaded. So, if you get their attention, you better grab it wherever you are!

When you get an opening, you must express yourself:

- Quickly
- Clearly
- Compellingly and
- Memorably

Create a sound bite, a descriptive message that you can deliver in less than 15 seconds when you meet new people. The purpose of a sound bite is to capture listeners' attention and give them information that will whet their appetite for more. Some refer to sound bites as "elevator speeches:" snappy, descriptions that can be rattled off in the time it takes an elevator to rise from the lobby to the fifth floor.

The more you say briefly, the better the sound bite. As theater impresario David Belasco said, "If you can't write your idea on the back of my calling card, you don't have a clear idea."

A sound bite is the opening that gets you to stage two. It's the first impression you make, an attention-grabbing device that will get you and your message noticed, remembered and repeated.

Your sound bite must be a grabber, a memorable message that makes contacts stop and listen, want to learn more about you and introduce you to their friends and colleagues. If it's short and gets their attention, it buys you more time to sell them. Your sound bite must be:

- *INTERESTING* enough to attract immediate *ATTENTION*,
- *POWERFUL* enough to be *REMEMBERED* and
- *CONVINCING* enough to *STIR* overloaded listeners into action.

In 10 to 15 seconds, your sound bite must explain:

(1) Who you are
(2) What you do and
(3) Why you make a difference.

Examples
The following are examples of effective sound bites:

(1) I teach business owners and salespeople how to make more money with less effort. I'm a business coach (C.J. Hayden).
(2) I used to weigh over 300 pounds. Now, I'm a size 8. I can teach you how to lose weight and keep it off. (Diet book author).
(3) I help people stay in focus, I'm an optometrist.
(4) I show people how to get unlimited free publicity. (Publicist).
(5) I make investors rich from small investments. (Investment broker).

(6) I turn your experiences, adventures and ideas into best-selling books. I'm a ghost writer. (Free-lance writer).

(7) I make the most delicious, mouth-watering and beautiful desserts for parties and special occasions (Pastry chef).

If you want to be a successful networker, prepare to vigorously promote yourself. Be ready to blow your own horn in such a way that listeners will remember the tune, but not consider you a blow hard. In the face of intense competition, distinguish yourself from the crowd and the best way to start is with a sound bite.

NETWORKING NUGGET

Several years ago, networking coach Sarah Michel made her "Perfecting Connecting" presentation at the United States Olympic Committee's Bi-annual Olympic Congress Conference at the Broadmoor Hotel in Colorado Springs. After she completed her session, Michel went the grand ballroom for the cocktail reception. She relaxed with a glass of red wine and talked to a woman in a beautiful cream-white suit, who attended her presentation. Out of the corner of her eye, she noticed Curt, a man who she had helped with his sound bite after her session, racing toward her. Suddenly, he picked her up and gave her a big bear hug, which cause her wine glass to tip and spill all over her companion's beautiful cream-white suit.

Curt immediately apologized, "I'm so sorry, but you're not going to believe what just happened. After I left your session, I went into the restroom and I mentally practiced my sound bite. As I was leaving, another man, who had also been in the rest room, asked me what I was doing at the conference. Remembering your instruction, I looked this guy straight in the eyes, stood tall and said, "I'm here to make some new connections and smoke out new opportunities where I can bring my 12 years of sales and marketing experience in the athletic sports and merchandising industry to a progressive company where I can really impact the bottom line."

The man then turned to Curt and said, "I'm the VP of New Business Development for NIKE. Would you like to grab a beer and talk about possible opportunities for you with Nike!"

Curt, who was floating on air, hugged Michel again, thanked her repeatedly and then shoved his business card into the hand of the woman in the stained white suit. "Send me the bill," he insisted. Then he smiled, hugged Michel again and went to meet the Nike VP!

Writing your sound bite

Before even attempting to write your sound bite, be sure that you clearly know what it is that you do. Most people don't know what they do, according to business expert Mitch Axelrod. "If I ask 100 people what they do, 90 of them will mumble, stumble and jumble. They've never really sat down and created a statement of what they do that is based on the results they achieved for the people they served." Axelrod explains. "While we think we know what we do, it's only from our own perspective. Our clients often perceive the benefits we provided quite differently. And they, and people like them, are usually the targets we're after."

Ask your customers or clients, "Why did you buy from me?" Ask even if you think you know. Inquire of 10, 15 or 30 customers or clients, why did you buy from or do business with me. At first some will be reluctant to tell you, but keep trying. Explain to them that their answers are important to you.

The answers you receive may surprise you. They may state reasons that you never would have suspected or imagined. They may reveal miscommunications, lack of clarity or just plain omissions or oversights by you.

After receiving your customers' or clients' input, incorporate what they told you in your sound bite. Then, when you subsequently give your sound bite, you will be telling those you meet the outcomes and results you have produced for you clients and customers, not the just naming the product your sell or the service you deliver. As a result, your pitch will more clearly explain the benefits that you can provide. It will also prevent listeners from putting a label on you, stop them from shackling you with their preconceived notions or lumping you in with all the other salespersons, professional speakers or construction worker they know.

> And while you're at it, ask those who didn't hire or buy from you the reasons why. It may not provide fodder for your sound bite, but their answers may point out what you did wrong that prevented you from getting their business. Often problems that their answers bring forth are easily correctible such as your not clearly having explained specific benefits they would have received from you. Unless you ask, you may have no other way to learn what you may have been doing wrong until it's too late.

Business coach C.J. Hayden believes that he best way to capture your listener's attention in a sound bite is first to state whom your message is intended to interest. In her sound bite, Hayden starts by saying that she teaches business owners and salespeople.

Next, state the benefit you provide, Hayden teaches. Tell listeners what is in it for them before you tell them what you do or how you do it. When you state your title or label first, it can position you in the mind of the listener. Upon hearing titles, many listeners immediately put people in a particular niche or slot and stop listening. If you open by saying that you are a lawyer, a listener might immediately connect you with unpleasant experiences they had with lawyers or with lawyer jokes and not listen to how you can help.

> Speaker, writer and trainer, Dave Sherman, "The Networking Guy," instructs clients to, "Have an engaging introduction—In this fast paced business world, people have less than ten seconds to engage others in a conversation. What most people say when asked, "What do you do," is the LAST thing they should ever say. Most people

respond with their name, their title and their company name. The challenge with this response is that NO ONE CARES WHAT THEY DO FOR A LIVING. People only care about what their company will do for them. If you can tell people how you can help them in 10 seconds or less, you will hear the three most beautiful words in the world, TELL ME MORE!

Always focus on the benefits—When people take the time to explain to others what they do, they typically focus on all the features of their product or service. This response is fine if they want to be like their competition. The only way to set yourself apart is by focusing on the benefits that your product or service provides. It's the benefits that people want to hear about because they are always concerned with "what's in it for them."

Give your sound bite in words that everyone can understand including those who are not in your industry. First, easily understood terms clearly convey to listeners precisely what you want. Second, in networking, the person you address may recommend you to others and if he/she does not fully understand what you said, he/she will not be able to clearly explain it to his/her contacts. Many of those who you approach will not be in your industry so avoid words that are specific to your industry because listeners may not understand them.

Make your sound bite an attention-grabbing introduction. Think of it as a commercial jingle selling you. Work it into letters, mailers, announcements, brochures, ads, e-mail signatures, forms, questionnaires and applications.

NETWORKING NUGGET

After months of going to networking meetings, having no luck and no favorable responses to his offerings, business advisor Mark LeBlanc tried a new method of introducing himself. Prior to this, he felt that he was repelling people with his various methods of introducing his products and services. So on this particular morning, when he got his opportunity, he simply stood up and said, "My name is Mark LeBlanc and I run a company called Small Business Success. I work with people who want to start a business and small business owners who want to grow their business."

The response was overwhelming. A number of attendees responded favorably and within 30 days LeBlanc got seven new clients. The floodgates opened and LeBlanc understood the importance of using the primary outcomes of his work in his sound bite. He now had come up with a defining statement that became the cornerstone of all of his marketing efforts, including his networking meetings. That morning became a turning point in LeBlanc's business!

1. First, write the first thoughts that come to mind. Don't worry how long they run or how much space they occupy. Be honest and truthful, but approach it from the bright side. Take your time; make as many attempts as necessary. When you have something down, (A) circle each descriptive word that you've written, (B) then list all of the circled words on a separate sheet, (C) place the listed words in the order of their importance, (D) question whether each of the selected words are the most descriptive and colorful words available and (E) if not, add or substitute more graphic, illustrative or hard-hitting words.

2. Draft a sound bite that runs one or two sentences. Begin with, and give prominence to, the most important words on your list. Although your sound bite should clearly and cleverly communicate your message, clarity is paramount. Don't sacrifice clarity for cleverness.

3. Mark LeBlanc suggests that you avoid the use of humor. "You may get people to laugh, when the real point is to be clear, congruent and consistent with your marketing message." However, others disagree and recommend humor provided it clearly gets your point across. They believe that humorous intros can be memorable.

4. Read the completed sound bite aloud several times and change whatever sounds awkward. Trust your ear. If you repeatedly trip over certain portions, change them to something more comfortable.

5. Underline the key words to be emphasized. Recite your sound bite aloud to test whether the emphasis on those words works. Experiment with differing rhythms and intonations. Recite your sound bite to others and get their input on both the content of your message and your delivery. Consider making changes that listeners suggest. Test it on different groups to get diverse reactions.

6. Recite the sound bite out loud until you believe it and feel comfortable delivering it. When you believe your sound bite, others will also. You'll also sound more confident and convincing.

7. Time how long it takes to deliver your sound bite. If it's more than 30 seconds, cut it to 30 seconds or less, then try to lop off another 10 to 15 seconds without weakening the message. Don't memorize your sound bite, instead picture the key words and reel them off in order as if you're descending a ladder.

8. Practice your sound bite in front of the mirror, in your car, in the shower. Audio and video tape yourself. Concentrate on looking sincere, enthusiastic and confident, but don't overdo it. Don't act, emote or be dramatic. Speak conversationally, with sincerity. Don't be a ham or a clown, be professional.

9. Practice, practice, practice … on your family, friends and pets. When you deliver your sound bite, imagine that your meeting the world's greatest networker, the President, Nelson Mandela, Steve Jobs, Oprah or and your business depends on your being booked on her show.

Delivering your message

Maintain eye contact and smile softly when you give your sound bite. Don't force it with some big, artificial grin. Smile warmly and convey confidence, assurance, conviction and sincerity. Show listeners that you're proud to deliver your message and that you believe in yourself and the benefits you can provide.

Project that you're an expert by speaking with

- Authority
- Excitement and
- Passion.

Excitement and passion are contagious. Listeners will sense your conviction, feed off it and want to share their belief in you with others. Football immortal Vince Lombardi reportedly said, "If you're not fired with enthusiasm, you'll be fired with enthusiasm!"

Repeat your sound bite at every opportunity. Practice, practice, practice! Always carry a stack of business cards to distribute when making your pitch. If you have brochures or other business materials, distribute them liberally.

Networking coach Sarah Michel has four rules for sound bites:
- Make them catchy but relatable, eliminate industry buzz words and abbreviations that don't translate well to others. If someone who has heard your drill just once can repeat it, watch out … you've just created your number one marketing tool and it's free!
- Establish your expertise up front. Be clear about what you're known for and what differentiates you from others who do what you do.
- Watch your body language. 93% of what people pay attention to is not _what_ you say, but _how_ you say it. During your delivery, are you smiling, do you make eye contact? Is your voice, pitch and rate of speech pleasant?
- Remember the 3-Foot rule. Anyone within three feet of you is a potential network contact. You never know where or when you'll get the opportunity to deliver your powerful introduction. It could be the opportunity of a lifetime!

Work your way around rooms, introduce yourself to new faces and continually give your sound bite. Repetition reinforces name recognition, brand identity and it builds confidence.

- Customize your sound bite for different audiences. For example, if you're at an auto dealers' meeting, sprinkle in terms relating to that industry like "on all cylinders," "out of gas" or "cruise control." Using your listeners' language breaks down barriers, lightens the mood and makes them feel that you're speaking directly to them. In doing so, you become one of them, at least for the time you're together.
- Prepare a back up sound bite. Be ready to ditch your standard message if it's inappropriate, if someone else in the group has a strikingly similar pitch or if your sound bite doesn't seem to be going over.
- Write "ad libs" that you can throw in to sound spontaneous. Remember, your main objective is to get your message across so if adjusting your sound bite improves your chances, be sure to go for it.
- Trust your instincts. You'll quickly learn how and when to alter your message and become adept at making changes based upon your instincts and observations. Work in references to hot news items, scandals or events that will make your sound bite more relevant, up to date.

Description of you, your product or service

If, after you've given your sound bite, listeners state that they want additional information, give them your brochure, other print materials or a verbal description. However, if you don't have or don't want to give out print materials, be prepared to verbally describe you, your product and services. Think of the description as the follow up or part 2 of your sound bite.

Often it's desirable to simply give your brochure or print materials those who request more information. It will give them your contact information and allow you to mingle and try to make more connections. However, when you have someone who truly seems interested, it may be worthwhile to spend a bit more time explaining what you do in the hope of building a tighter relationship. Use your instincts.

If listeners do not request additional information, ask if they would like copies of your brochure or print materials. Wait to be asked before delivering a verbal description of you, your product or services or you could come across as overly pushy and aggressive. Don't volunteer because you could kill off all chances of further contact.

A verbal description can run longer than the 10 to 15 second sound bite, but try to keep it between 15 to 30 seconds. Be considerate of your listeners. They have other things to do, many have short attention spans or are there to circulate and make contacts, so keep the description of your product or services short and sweet. When you finish giving your description, ask if they would like you to send or email them more information.

Think of your description as a mini brochure that explains the benefits you provide. Be specific. Structure your description by listing each benefit that you provide in the order of its importance. List no more than seven benefits, but if your business offers more, as the last item state that you provide additional benefits. Only identify the additional items if asked and then, describe each item in just a few words.

The most common problem with descriptions of yourself, your product or service is lack of clarity. When you know a subject intimately, it's easy to assume that everyone else understands it. As a result, we tend to use terms specific to our industries and expect others to understand them, which may not be true.

In describing what you do, be extremely specific. Avoid generalized terms that may create misunderstandings. If you're an accountant, state that you prepare tax returns, appear with clients at IRS audits and prepare financial statements. Be specific! From your description, people should be able to fully understand what they will be getting from you.

Business cards

Like your sound bite, your business card is a vital tool in your networking package. Unlike sound bites, business cards should contain all of your contact information so the people you meet can easily get in touch with you. Business cards are reminders: they are intended to jog a contact's memory when he/she comes across your card weeks, months or even years after you met. They must provide the information necessary to contact you.

The front of your business card should include:

- Your name and the name of your business
- An explanation of what you do: colonial U.S. furniture dealer, pet portrait photographer, wallpaper hanger. Clarity is essential because contacts may have collected dozens of cards at an event and must be able to ascertain simply by looking at your card precisely what you do.
- The addresses at which you wish to be contacted by postal mail and/or email
- Your telephone, cellular telephone and/or fax numbers and
- Your Web site address.

Your card can also include your position or official title, logo, sound bite, motto or a short slogan. Many people use both sides of their business cards. The backs of cards can provide more information about what you do, testimonials, maps and other graphic works.

Business cards saves everyone time and energy because they quickly and easily convey important information that can be permanently filed at a later time. Since business cards are inexpensive advertisements, they should be distributed liberally to whomever you meet.

Design your cards in a style that will reflect the impression you want to convey. Make it distinctive, yet appropriate. Avoid the temptation to clutter your card with so much information that it is difficult to read. If you need space, use both sides. However, since contacts frequently write information on the back of business cards, you may want to print your information on only one side of your card.

Before designing your business card, leaf through all the cards that you've collected. Identify features, styles and that you appeal to you and that you believe will work for you. Consider that the person you provide your business card to might want to take notes on your card. When you have your cards printed, use a non-glossy finish on the back to make your cards easier to write on.

Contact list, calendar and writing materials

Don't leave home without them. Contact lists, calendars and writing materials are the networkers' stock in trade. When you make a new contact, few things are as impressive as coming up with a resource they need and immediately giving the new contact all of the match's contact information. And now, the wide availability of mobile devices has made carrying this information both easy and fun.

Carrying your calendar with you allows you to arrange appointments on the spot. You can quickly book lunch or make an appointment with a great new contact and avoid the electronic barriers that can make trying to connect so frustrating.

Stash pens, pencils and pads everywhere. Carry them in your pockets, purses, briefcases, glove compartments, in every room in hour home and office. Always be prepared to capture a name, address or important information.

Mobile devices contain contact lists, calendars and memo applications in one small, tidy package. With these devices, you can instantly beam addresses, contact and schedule information to contacts devices. Some also have digital audio recorders that let you record brief information, such as addresses and phone numbers, for later use. An additional benefit of a mobile device is that you can also snap their photo and attach it to their record. Use the contact list and calendar application provided in your mobile device or use one of the many CRM (Contact Relationship Management) systems that are now available – many with mobile apps to supercharge your networking activities.

Expertise

As we've previously discussed and will discuss further, to build and maintain a successful network you must be an expert. Expertise must be an integral part of your networking tool kit; you can't get far without it.

If you can flawlessly deliver a snappy sound bite, the most compelling description and have the best of all the rest, you ultimately need expertise. Without expertise you have little of lasting value to give to your network partners. Without expertise you won't be able to contribute, provide benefits, pay your own way or hold your own and eventually those you want to deal with will no longer want you.

★☆★ Action steps ★☆★

---

1. Write a killer sound bite that you can deliver in 30 seconds.

_____

_____

_____

2. Write a killer sound bite that you can deliver in 15 seconds.

_____

_____

_____

3. Write a verbal description of your product or service that you can deliver in 30 seconds or less.

_____

_____

_____

4. List the items to be included on your business card.

_____

_____

_____

CHAPTER 7

APPROACHING TARGETS

"Have a bias toward action—let's see something happen now. You can break that big plan into small steps and take the first step right away."
—**Richard Thalheimer**, The Sharper Image Founder

This chapter will cover:
- ❑ *Know your purpose*
- ❑ *Your appearance*
- ❑ *Be considerate*
- ❑ *Anatomy of a networking event*
- ❑ *Building relationships*
- ❑ *Talking business*

It's a steamy, summer Sunday afternoon. You've been working like a dog in the yard in the blazing sun to round up mountains of junk that you've been stashing and trying to ignore for years. After a few hours, you run out of garbage bags and dash down to the store for a fresh supply.

You find the bags quickly and as you wait to pay, you spot the agent for that fabulous building where you've been dying to move your office. Although you've phoned her dozens of times, she seldom calls back and when she does, it's always too late, the space has been rented. Normally, you would say hello, make small talk and ask if any vacancies might be coming up. Typically, you would use this chance meeting to turn on the charm and try to talk her into giving you advance notice of upcoming vacancies. But you're sweaty, smelly and look like a slob. As much as you want to get into that building, you're afraid that your appearance would permanently kill your kill your chances. So you bow your head, turn away, pay for the bags and duck out of the store on the double … letting the opportunity pass.

Smart networkers are always prepared to network. They know that at any time, at any place, they could meet someone they know or whom they would like to get to know. So whenever they're out, they're always ready, they are never caught unprepared. Savvy networkers never lose sight of their purpose, they what they want, and they are always neat, well groomed and appropriately dressed. Successful networkers understand the importance of making the best impression and they always expect and are prepared for the unexpected.

Know your purpose

Whether you go to the store, to the Elks Club or to the White House, know your purpose. Know why you're there and exactly what you hope to achieve. Never leave anything to chance or wing it; always be ready to give your best.

Act appropriately under the circumstances and understand that you never know who is looking you, watching you and how that is going to affect you in the future.

NETWORKING NUGGET

The non-stop temptations plague workers in the hotel-casino industry. They are continually enticed by gambling, sumptuous dinning, elaborate receptions, free-flowing bars, spectacular shows, expense accounts and gorgeous women. It challenges even the most saintly to stay focused. Many fall victim, lose their perspective and forget that their companies sent them to these amidst these enticements to meet people and get business.

When Neil Mullanaphy was the sales manager at a major Atlantic City hotel-casino, the Hotel and Visitors Authority hired him to be the national sales manager for the opening of its new convention center. Mullanaphy learned that he was selected for his new position because for five or six years, the Authority's top brass had observed him at trade shows, hospitality functions and other events. They noticed his ability to network, work a room and to keep his focus while so many of his colleagues strayed … and the Authority's honchos remembered it.

Mullenaphy remained with the Authority for seven years, which gave him the credentials to get a job as Director of Trade Show and Association Sale as Las Vegas' Mandalay Bay Hotel and now acting President & CEO of the Puerto Rico Convention Bureau. In addition, the woman who hired Mullenaphy at Mandalay Bay knew him from industry events that he attended for the Authority and his excellent reputation preceded his job application.

Whether you know it or know, people are always watching you. They're monitoring you appearance, demeanor, focus and resolve. They're making judgments about you, judgments that could affect your life.

Expect the unexpected. Know that when you least expect it you will encounter someone or something that can change everything. The next time you go to the movies, be prepared to see that elusive guy who never returns your calls. When see him, be ready to strut your stuff. When that moment comes, you may decide that it would be inappropriate to pitch and that it may be wiser to just say hello. But be prepared because he just might ask for what you were polite enough to withhold.

Be considerate

We've all been on the receiving end of bull rushes from relentless pursuers who simply refuse to take no for an answer. These persistent characters have such intense focus, such single-minded insensitivity that you can't shake them. They seem dauntless, impervious to clear rejections and you have to virtually hit them over the head to ward them off.

In addition, they always catch you at the most inconvenient or inappropriate times. They deliberately call while you're eating or busy with others. They work weddings, funerals and social affairs like barracudas swimming in well-stocked waters. Their purpose is to wear you down and it frequently works. Sometimes you buy from or deal with them just to get them off your back, but in most cases, you would rather die than give them a dime. And those who deal with them, only do so once because who would want to repeat such unpleasant experiences?

> Be considerate of contacts. Don't intrude or overstay your welcome. "People who overtly network or overtly try to sell themselves to others are usually not very successful," Robert Iger, Chairman of the Walt Disney Company told us. "You have to be ambitious, but you cannot wear ambition on your sleeve. Plus, you cannot "press" too hard. It's always better to sell yourself with deeds than with blatant salesmanship. Also, you have to wait for the opportunity to present itself and then pounce on it when it comes. People who try to create opportunities look too opportunistic."

Networking events

Before you attend a networking event:

- Know your purpose. Clearly define what you hope to accomplish and set concrete goals. Challenge yourself. Decide whether you want three catering jobs, get recommendations on a new printer or find out which French classes you should attend?

- Decide how many people you want to meet. Do you want to find three people who hire speakers, three skate board experts or seven prospects for your book club. Identify precisely who you hope to meet and have a back up list.

- Set financial goals. Put precise dollar figures on the business you hope to generate. Tell your projections to friends; it will increase your resolve and help them to spot leads and opportunities for you.
- Determine what you want to learn. Clearly identify the areas where you need more knowledge and ask those you meet for their ideas of the best ways to attain it.
- Have a list of questions that you can ask other attendees, speakers or members of the host organization. For example, why are you here? What are you working on? What books do you recommend? Which people should I meet?
- Allow yourself to have fun. Keep in mind that networking events are not all business; they have a social component. So make it a point to have fun and enjoy yourself. When you are having fun people will be attracted to you and you will network more successfully.

Business expertise. As we've previously said, in order to successfully network, you must know your stuff, you must be an expert. You need business expertise. Business expertise is not just a one-time accumulation of knowledge that once attained need not be further maintained. To the contrary, business expertise is a continuing process of learning, keeping up and testing the frontiers, the outer limits of your industry. To do business with the best, you can't merely be up to speed, you must be in the vanguard, among the elite, at the front of the pack.

If you go to an event and can't promptly provide great answers to inquiries about your interests, you're committing networking suicide. You're placing a big black mark next to your name, on your reputation, which those present will remember and may report to their friends. Overcoming negative impressions is murder because most people won't give you a second chance; they won't waste their time with someone who has already proven unworthy.

So, if you're going to network, know your stuff and be able to clearly articulate it. View every question an opportunity and be ready to make the most of each.

Personal expertise. Increase your knowledge by getting into the habit of constantly reading. Knowledge is power. Read everything: national and local newspapers, magazines and a wide variety of books. Read about your business, your interests, other people's businesses and their interests as well as totally new subjects. Expand your horizons.

Reading places deposits in your knowledge bank and it yields interest that compounds constantly. Hellen Davis, CEO of Indaba Training Specialists, Inc. makes it a point to read the Wall Street Journal and USA Today in the morning before she attends networking events. Davis feels that having the latest business and national news at her fingertips makes her more interesting, which enhances her ability to make a wide range of contacts that can develop into strong relationships.

Your appearance

People judge you by your appearance even if they don't know or won't admit to it, their reactions are deeply ingrained. Like it or not, many decisions are influenced by your appearance, what you wear, how you look and how you present yourself, so do yourself a favor and always try to look your best.

Dress appropriately. Wear clothing that will not offend the people you hope to meet. If you meet with a banker who wears a suit, you don't also have to wear a suit, but look neat, clean and well groomed if you want to get that loan. If a company has "casual Friday, your business suit will be inappropriate. When you have to appear in court, don't wear shorts or your old, stained car-washing outfit. As Jill says, "If you want to wear shorts, go to the beach."

- If you plan to play tennis, wear whites
- If you want to weld, wear protective goggles
- If you hope to do business, dress for business

Dress appropriately for the occasion. Whites for tennis honor tradition, welding goggles provide safety and business clothing shows respect. When your appearance is inappropriate, it's often be interpreted as a sign of disrespect. It also can be read as insensitivity or simply that you don't care enough to make an effort to be neat, clean and properly dressed

People avoid those who offend their values. So be smart, give them what makes them comfortable and what will put them at ease. If you do, you will be more likely to get what you want.

According to an old adage, it's better to overdress than underdress. Although that rule may no longer hold with many of today's youth-oriented companies, it's still generally true. When in doubt, dress up, rather than down. It never hurts to look your best, but it certainly could hurt to look less than your best.

Before you attend networking events, plan what you're going to wear. Examine it to be sure that it's clean, well pressed and in good condition. When you select your networking attire, it's more important not to offend, than it is to impress.

> At networking most events, you'll find yourself physically close to others so be sure that you don't offend. Get a good haircut, be clean, well groomed and brush your teeth. Avoid drinking coffee, it leaves a stale, unpleasant and long-lasting odor. Talking tends to dry your mouth so drink lots of water. Don't be afraid to tote a small bottle of water, it's totally acceptable at most networking events.

Business cards

Carry plenty of business cards with you so you can quickly hand them out. It's amazing how many people go to business meetings and networking events without business cards. The great networkers always keep a stack of their business cards close at hand: when they're at the beach, on their boat or working out. They're never without them and neither should you.

If contacts say that you and their friend would make a good match, give them two business cards: one for them and the other for their friend. If they give you their business card, write on the back the name and contact information for their friend, ask if you can call and use their name.

Anatomy of a networking event

When you go to a networking event, your networking opportunities begin as soon as you get out of the car, the subway or off the bus. Start conversations with people who enter the building with you, talk to those who are searching for directions or who press the same elevator button. Being pleasant, warm and friendly never hurts; it doesn't cost a thing, but it can produce huge returns.

When you get to the event, head straight for the reception table. Sign in, get your nametag and whatever materials are being distributed. If there is a line or people gathered by the reception table, begin networking by introducing yourself to those nearby. Start a conversation by finding out who they are and telling them how much you're looking forward to the event. After you've made your first contact, it's usually easier to meet others.

Don't ignore reception desk workers. Often, they are volunteers or key people in the host organization. They may even be the event organizers or hosts. Talking with reception desk workers is networking; it's extending you contact base and building relationships. So say hello and thank them because they are frequently ignored or treated indifferently. They will appreciate and remember your kindness.

Reception desk workers frequently assist with various chores during the event and can help you throughout the event. They often act as official greeters for the host organizations and part of that job may be to make introductions. Don't be afraid to ask greeters or desk workers for help or to introduce you to key people.

Arrive early

Networking expert Dave Sherman believes that over 90 percent of those who attend networking events feel uncomfortable to some extent. To overcome your discomfort, he recommends that you arrive at networking events 15 minutes early. "I know, I know." Sherman states, "Only geeks show up early. Not true! I prefer to believe the adage that 'The early bird gets the worm.'"

By arriving early, you have the opportunity the chance to meet the people who put on the event before they're inundated with other guests and duties. Usually, they are the movers and shakers of the sponsor organization and are the best folks to connect with, especially if you're new to the organization.

NETWORKING NUGGET

Event organizers know who's who at their events. They also know the movers and shakers as well as the hangers on, who should be avoided. When Hellen Davis, CEO of Indaba Training Systems, Inc., arrives at an event, she finds the promoters or hosts of the event to introduce herself. After explaining who she is, she asks, "If you were me, who would you want to meet?" When they name names, Davis asks them to introduce her. "It's remarkable," she explained, "They (organizers and/or promoters) can interrupt any one at any time and when they interrupt conversations to introduce me, it elevates my status and make me seem more important."

Another reason to show up early is because it's easier to start networking with the 5-10 people who are already present than with the 50-100 who will soon arrive. It's hard to walk into a room filled with people and to jump right into your networking mode. When fewer attendees are on hand, you can warm up slowly. Once you break the ice and start talking, it becomes easier and more comfortable to chat with others. People you approach often appreciate your interest in them and in turn will become more comfortable and forthcoming with you.

If your nametag isn't preprinted, sign it legibly and print your name in large letters that everyone can read. Some attendees won't be wearing their glasses so help them to identify you by writing your name clearly. Wear it where it can be easily seen.

At events sponsored by Executive Moms, a New York City organization for women who balance their careers as business executives with being mothers, attendees wear two nametags. One nametag has the woman's name and where she resides while the other lists the names and ages of her children. The two nametags increase the opportunities for the women at the events to talk, interact and build relationships, according to Marisa Thalberg, Vice President, Global Digital Marketing at The Estee Lauder Companies and Executive Mom's Founder and President.

After putting on their nametags, some people like to step to the side to survey the room before they venture further. Locate the food area because it's an excellent place to socialize. Sooner or later, everyone at events wanders over to the food area where the atmosphere is more relaxed. As you walk toward the food area, look for opportunities to network.

People like to hang around food areas. It gives them a break. Around food, most people tend to be more open and at ease. Just the mere presence of food loosens them up. Since the atmosphere around the food isn't as charged, it's easier to strike up conversations with openings such as, "Isn't the Danish great?" "Oh, those egg rolls look good," or "Oh well, I know I shouldn't ... but."

Rosters
If the sponsor provides a roster of attendees, check the names listed to identify who you would like to meet and who you know. Most rosters are handed out

when you sign in, so study them as soon as you get the chance. If you can, obtain and read the roster in advance.

Some rosters provide information about the attendees and it's surprising how much of it will come to mind when you meet that person face-to-face. When you go to trade shows and large conferences, get a list of attendees and exhibitors before hand and the schedule of when you can attend the exhibits.

Scan the main areas to see where everyone congregates. Discover whether they are moving around or standing in groups and where the energy is. If people all gather at a certain place, try to discover what is going on. Ask someone, "Why is everyone standing over there?" It's good way to start a conversation.

Move in the direction of the people and the energy. If you see someone alone, introduce yourself and begin to network.

Jill Lublin advises people to "act like a butterfly." When you meet friends at events, it is not the appropriate time to involve yourselves in prolonged discussions that go into the intimate details of their lives. It's the time to network, to get down to business. When Jill sees someone she knows at a networking event, she simply says hello and asks how he/she is without getting into a deep conversation. Then she moves on. With people she doesn't know, Jill invests more time.

Jill believes that networking events are primarily to meet new people. Although she loves the social aspects of seeing old friends, Jill understands that the purpose of networking events is to make new contacts.

If Jill knows three people in a group of three, she will say hello to the two she knows and introduce herself to the person she doesn't know. At networking events, Jill always speaks and introduces herself first because so may attendees are uncomfortable introducing themselves, some even freeze up.

Greet and be cordial to the people you know, but concentrate on meeting new people. If you want to make new contacts, don't sit or hang out with friends or business associates, but seek out new faces and get to meet them.

Approaching others

Approach people when your eyes meet or they smile at you and hold their smile. Try to connect with people who communicate with vibrancy and enthusiasm and seem interested and excited. Look for energy and vitality.

Before approaching others, look for body language that reveals if they are open to talking or not interested. Those with their arms crossed over their torso, who are unsmiling, looking around nervously or who step back when you approach are not open. People who are not into talking with you won't acknowledge you or will acknowledge you briefly, unsmilingly and then quickly turn or step away. Frequently, they'll give you a quick, sharp nod. They're sending out "Do not approach" signals. Do what they ask, leave them alone! If they don't want to talk, simply smile pleasantly and move on.

People who are open to talking to you will usually smile, nod, make an opening comment or introduce themselves. Look at their eyes, if they hold your gaze or don't seem to look straight through you, continue your approach. Open people hug, laugh, smile, look people straight in the eyes and lean forward toward the person they're talking with.

Jill likes to approach people when they're standing alone because it usually means that they don't know what to do next. Although she doesn't spend a lot of time with them, she tries to make them comfortable. Jill will also escort them over to groups that she feels she can enter and be a part of.

When people are in a group, read the looks and gestures of the group members to determine if you're welcome. If members of a group acknowledge you or smile or nod to you, smile or nod back. Introduce yourself only if it doesn't interrupt the conversation and even then, be brief. Give your sound bite. If you feel that you're not welcome in their conversation, simply smile and slip away.

When you approach a group that is involved in conversation:

- Remain silent until you can figure out what they are discussing
- Listen and remain silent until you have something that is both relevant and of value to add, otherwise don't speak
- Irrelevant and/or valueless comments are rude interruptions that most people resent.

Often, it pays to position yourself to the side of a group where you can eavesdrop on their conversation. After listening for a while, you may find that you're not interested in talking with them. In addition, you could learn something that would ease your entry into the group or that would smooth your approach when you subsequently come across group members during the event.

When someone you would like to meet is surrounded and it's hard to approach, don't be intimidated. Be patient and wait your turn because most people are usually approachable, you just may have to wait.

Speakers at events can be hard to reach. If, after patiently waiting, you still have not gotten your chance, see if the speakers have "guards" or people escorting them. If so, tell their escorts, "I'd love to speak with Jane, when is the best time to contact her?" Sometimes the escorts will tell you, "Just wait here," and will stand with you in such a way that the speaker will notice and give you your chance.

Speakers and celebrities are always haunted by attendees insist on asking them a million questions and refusing to relinquish the floor. If you wait patiently, speaker will frequently notice and cut short the hanger on.

Jill doesn't believe in preplanning opening gambits because she considers them insincere and transparent. "People sense and resent insincerity, they know its manipulative and it turns them off." Instead, Jill gives her sound bite, relies on her instincts and opens by complimenting a pretty outfit (only when she means it) or commenting on something she observed. The only thing Jill preplans, she stresses, is what she says about her business. Nothing else is planned.

NETWORKING NUGGET

When Jill attends networking events, she wears outfits with two side pockets. In her right pocket, she keeps her business cards, which she liberally hands out. In her left pocket, she puts the business cards she receives from others. On the rare occasion when she wears an outfit that doesn't have two side pockets, she carries a compartmentalized holder that has separate sections for her book, business cards, postcards, marketing materials and other people's cards.

When Jill receives other people's business cards, she writes notes on their cards before putting them in her pocket or holder, even if they are still present. Jill feels that most people are flattered that she is interested and organized enough to note information about them on the back of their card. However, if you feel uncomfortable, say something like, "Let me write this down so I won't forget."

- When you meet people try hard to remember their names. To improve your ability to remember names, see Chapter 14, Special Tactics, Remembering names. Repeat contacts' names: find ways to work them in to conversations and call them by name when you speak and subsequently see them.

- Look for opportunities to give genuine compliments. Compliments are great icebreakers, especially those that are astute. However, don't give compliments when you don't mean them or the word will soon circulate and your believability quotient will crash. Tell contacts when you enjoyed what they said, agreed with they wrote, admired what they did or even liked what they wore.

If you consistently remember people's names and give sincere compliments, they will warm to you and networking will become easier and more productive.

- Circulate and look for opportunities to meet people who you don't know. Networking events present opportunities to make new contacts so don't cling to your friends or those with whom you work. Move around and make new contacts that could grow into meaningful relationship.

Leaving a group

People who enter a group don't have to stay in the conversation. You can excuse yourself at any time, but prepare an exit strategy. Before the event, think of a few basic lines that will let you politely slip out of a conversation without appearing to be rude. For example, you smile and simply say, "I need to get a drink," "I need to say hello to someone" or "Oh, I need to coordinate my ride home" and then walk away. And, no matter how badly you want to leave the group, never be discourteous or overly abrupt.

Unlike most people in the world, we Americans aren't taught to separate social and business situations. As a result, in the US, business talk is always considered appropriate, which in certain situations can cause problems. For example, in social situations, it's polite to remain in conversations that no longer involve you and leaving the conversation could be considered rude. On the other hand, in business situations, staying in conversations that no longer involve you is rude.

At networking events, when a new person enters the conversation and the subject changes so that it no longer concerns or is about you, move on. By remaining in the conversation, you can dampen the dynamic, sap the energy and inhibit the creation of new and meaningful dialogs. At that point, when it no longer involves you, politely say goodbye and leave. If you want to make a specific plan, say, "It's been great talking to you, should I call you next week, what day would be good?" And then leave. If you don't want any further contact, say "It was nice seeing you, I'll look forward to seeing you at the next event."

Many people find networking events uncomfortable and don't know how to act. Try to be kind, understanding and compassionate, but remember your purpose. Excusing yourself from unproductive conversations may be uncomfortable, but it is necessary. At networking events, you're there for business, not to socialize or to nurse uncomfortable people.

Building relationships

Remember your purpose. When you approach targets, your primary purpose is to make contacts that can bloom into strong relationships, not to sell your product or service.

Networking and relationship building, like most good things, doesn't happen instantly, it takes time. It must be developed in stages, nurtured, step-by-step, with patience, care and persistence. Relationship building starts the moment you see a target, even before you say a word or stick out your hand and say hello.

Never underestimate the impact of a first impression and how long it lasts. People long remember initial contacts and those impressions affect the manner in which they deal with you. So make a strong initial impression. Stand tall, smile, look directly at your target and offer your hand. Don't try to bowl him/ her over, just try to connect.

Don't sell, build. Approach targets with the intention of getting to know them, building friendships and solid relationships. When you meet and get to know people, think what you can do for them and with whom you can match them. Can you give them leads or connect them with someone in your network?

Be selective in choosing your targets because you only have limited time and resources. Develop your instincts to hone in on targets with the best potential and avoid those who only want to take from you. These people have few good contacts and want entrée to your network partners.

Business expert Mitch Axelrod has developed a system that he calls "Rejection-Proof Networking." The core of his system, which Mitch has refined over a 20-year period, is explained below.

NETWORKING NUGGET

In 1982, when Mitch was a financial planner, he wanted million dollar clients. So he developed a 5-step approach that he called "Take a Millionaire to Lunch." Using this approach, he increased his income 600% in two years—from $16,000 in 1982 to $100,000 in 1984. From 1990 to 1995, he used his method again in a different business and increased his fees by 1000%. Mitch's approach is:

1. List your 20 best centers of influence!

List the names of the 20 people you know who could help you most. Don't pre-judge, pre-qualify or pre-determine if they will help you. Aim high! You can also make a second list of the wealthiest people you know.

2. Categorize each person as an A, B, or C resource.

A= Absolutely can help

B= Better than 50/50 chance

C= Can; maybe, but maybe not!

3. Send a letter to or call your A List. Ask them to meet you in person for 15 minutes.

Tell them, "I value your opinion. I trust you to tell me the truth. I'd like your advice, counsel and help." Be genuine, sincere and really mean it! Don't even think about trying to sell them anything. You want their advice and help. Period! Their help will be worth a small fortune to you.

4. When you meet them, explain What—Why—Who—How—Where.

What—you are doing and what your goals are. Be clear about what you want and where you want to go.

Why—you decided to do what you're doing. Demonstrate your passion and commitment.

Who—you are looking to reach. Make a list of the type of people who would be in the best position to further your quest and give you access to their resources and relationships.

How—you want help. Describe the resources, relationships and results you are looking for. Be as detailed as you can.

Where—should I go next? Where can you send me to get what I'm looking for?

5. Now, ask one or all of these BIG questions:

"What would you do if you were me?"

"What advice would you give your best friend?"

"How would you handle this situation?"

"Who can I talk to - where should I go from here?"

Keep in mind. Most people want to help. If you're courageous and determined enough to ask, you will find the help you need. When people are approached to sign up for, or buy into something, they often get defensive and put up their guard. If they don't buy the product or service, they may find it awkward to recommend it or the person who offered it. Their sales resistance will make it harder for them to be a networking resource for you.

When making a request of a contact, be direct and specific. State what you need clearly and descriptively. Be honest and up front about what you want and don't be greedy. Be grateful for every effort made in your behalf.

Talking business

After you develop a relationship with a contact, don't talk business until you're absolutely certain that your contact will be receptive. If you feel that asking for help would kill the relationship, back off and live to fight another day. Ideally, by the time you ask for help, you will have given your new contact leads or connected him/her with your network partners.

When you're ready:

- Be direct and totally honest
- Explain precisely what you need
- State exactly how your contact can help
- Inquire if your contact knows others who might help
- Point out what you have to offer
- Stress the importance of your contact's help
- If your contact gives you a lead, request permission to use his/her name
- Ask how you can repay or help your contact
- Express your gratitude for your contact's help

Most contacts are realists who understand the reciprocal nature of business. If they like you, owe you, or better yet, if they believe in you, they'll be happy to recommend you. It's good business and if you do well, it will make them look good. When you approach contacts:

- Try to get three leads. Expect your contacts to be cautious until they're convinced that you consistently deliver high-quality work
- Be patient and persistent
- Ask for the chance to prove yourself and
- Take less, or nothing at all, to get your foot in the door.

Referral fees

Clarify in advance whether your contacts expect referral fees. If they do, clarify exactly how much they want. Quantify the amount or percentage they expect and make sure that you are both in full agreement. In some businesses and localities, referral fees are unethical. Since the rules vary from place to place, check out what's acceptable where you transact that business.

When you get business via a referral, find ways to show your appreciation you're your contact can't or won't accept a referral fee, consider giving a gift, a gift certificate, tickets to an event, a charitable contribution or perform extra or personal work for them to say thanks. Gestures of gratitude are greatly appreciated and are good business.

★☆★ Action steps ★☆★

1. Write three icebreakers to start a conversation with a stranger.

_____

_____

_____

2. Write three exit lines to leave a conversation that is no longer productive.

_____

_____

_____

3. List the names of 20 people you know who could help you the most.

_____

_____

_____

4. Compose a letter asking the 20 people on you list to meet you for 15 minutes.

_____

_____

_____

CHAPTER 8

ORGANIZED
NETWORKING GROUPS

"We all have these places where shy humiliations
gambol on sunny afternoons."
—Poet **W.H. Auden**

This chapter will cover:
❑ *Types of networking groups*
❑ *Network Associates*
❑ *Circles of Eight*
❑ *The Hubble Group*
❑ *Network Professional, Inc.*
❑ *eWomenNetwork*

Whenever people congregate, networking opportunities exist. Therefore, most good networkers join groups where they can make new contacts and incorporate them into their networks. Groups are ideal for networking because they bring together like-minded individuals who frequently share common backgrounds, interests and goals. Through groups, networkers can expand their reach and make connections with those it might otherwise take them considerably longer to meet. As a result, many accomplished networkers concentrate the bulk of their networking efforts on groups.

Originally, many of the groups where people now network were not organized to facilitate networking. However, networking became such an integral part of their members' interactions that many of them added networking sessions or events as a significant part of their programming. Usually, these groups were started to promote business, social, community, religious, charitable or other endeavors. Such groups can include trade associations to your Wednesday night card game, your bowling team as well as business, social, religious, community, charitable and service organizations. They also can include youth, recreational and athletic teams, fraternities, sororities and alumni organizations.

Trade and industry associations provide outstanding networking opportunities. They were founded to promote the interests of specific industries and their members. A key mission of these associations is to lobby for legislation that will help the industry and defeat proposals that might do it harm. Trade associations also provide forums for the education and welfare of its members and, at many of these forums, association members meet fellow members, exhibit their wares, discuss mutual problems and provide help for one another via networking. Although trade and industry associations were not founded as networking organizations, they have evolved into networking Meccas.

In addition to trade associations, other major networking organizations include business organizations such as Chambers of Commerce, CEO Space, Consulting Alliance (the Entrepreneual Edge) and Shared Vision Network. Service organizations—which include the Masons, Kiwanis, Elks, Lions and Rotary Clubs and Soroptimists—also provide ideal venues for networking.

Recently, groups popped up everywhere that exist primarily to help their members network; we call these organized networking groups or network focused groups. Large network focused groups include national organizations such as eWomenNetwork, LeTip International, Inc. BNI International (almost 7,000 chapters internationally, over 145,000 members) and Ali Lassen's Leads Club (5,500 members, 400 chapters) to name just a few. These organizations have local chapters and also hold national meetings, conventions and training sessions.

In addition, numerous local networking groups operate throughout the country. Some of these groups may be affiliated with national, state or other local organizations, but many are simply single units that were created to facilitate the building of relationships on a wide range of interests. Besides those dedicated to business, other networking groups focus on interests that range from dating to promoting book sales.

Network groups require an investment of time and money, but most members consider them to be wise investments in themselves.

Group Profiles

Since so many organized networking groups exist, it's simply impossible to describe them all. Therefore, we selected five network-focused groups to provide a sampling of the range of networking groups, their approaches and how they operate. In profiling these groups, our intention was to provide a representative cross section of networking groups to illustrate what groups can offer and how they operate.

One or more of these groups, or your own version of them, may be ideal for you for someone you know. The groups profiled are:

- Network Associates, Inc.
- Caterina Rando's Circle of Eight
- The Hubbel Group
- AmSpirit Business Connections and
- eWomenNetwork.

Network Associates

Steve Krauser runs seven networking groups in New York and New Jersey under the banner of Network Associates. Harvey Krauser operates four Network Associates' groups in Florida. In the following when we use the name Krauser, we will be referring to Steve Krauser.

Each group Network Associates' group has an average of 20 to 25 members, men and women, who pay an annual $2,000 fee. Each group meets once a month. They meet a regularly scheduled day, such as the first Tuesday of the month, and at a set time like 8 to 10 A.M. Meetings are held at a conference hall and members sit around circular tables. Krauser presides from the front of the room.

In addition to running meetings, Krauser also calls members randomly to talk or set up times when he can visit them at their places of business. He likes to see their operation and discuss the state of their business. "This is a member-directed organization," Krauser points out. "Their input and feedback is very important to me." He sees his job as making sure that the flame is always burning and he always tries to be up beat and positive with members.

Except for one group, which is specific to the media and entertainment industry, each Network Associates' group is separate and noncompetitive. No two people from the same industry classification who theoretically compete can be members of a Network Associates' group. "A free exchange of information and ideas is powerful. And how can you have a free exchange of information and ideas if a competitor is sitting in the room with you?" Krauser asks.

In a group, the career fields represented might include a stock broker, computer consultant, real estate and personal injury attorney, mortgage banker, telephone system consultant, video teleconferencing expert, water purification system expert, property and casualty insurance broker, life and health insurance broker, graphic designer, accountant, etc. Members join Network Associates as businesses, which enables more than one member of a business to attend meetings.

Guests

To insure a good mix, Krauser regularly asks members to identify businesses that are not represented in the group and whether representatives of those industries should be invited to meetings as guests? If the group members want more information about that industry, Krauser ask them to "identify people they know, feel comfortable with and who understand the concept of relationship-driven sales, as opposed to transactional sales. When there are certain industry classifications that are in the chain of referral that need to be filled, we call upon the members to help us fill those gaps," Krauser explained. Occasionally, a guest will host a meeting at his or her place of business.

Early each year, Krauser posts the schedule of meetings for the year. Prior to each meeting, he sends out memos reminding members about the meeting and informing them about the program so that they can prepare. "You can't walk into any meeting today and wing it. You have to be prepared! And, that holds true with networking meetings," Krauser stressed.

Krauser also finds out if members are planning to bring a guest to the next meeting. If so, he asks the member to send him information about the invitee. Then he will send the guest a formal invitation listing all pertinent information such as the meeting date, time and place.

Guests must be invited to meetings. Unlike other networking groups, guests are not welcome to show up uninvited. "This is a very exclusive business development club. You must be invited," Krauser said. "Guests are invited only if it will be a mutually beneficial relationship. They must get something out of it, but they must also give something back to the membership. Otherwise, the chain of opportunity breaks down."

To join a Network Associates' group, candidates must first attend two meetings as guests. Krauser and the Business Advisory Council, which consists of Krauser and select members, must approve new members. The size of the Business Advisory Councils vary from group to group, but members must have been in the group for a while, understand the process and have a vested interest in the organization's growth and development.

New members are selected on the basis of what they bring to the table. For instance, are they a compatible business, can they make contributions that would benefit other group members, do candidate have good personalities and will they be positive additions? Any one member can veto a candidate for membership in the group. If members miss too many meetings, they will be dropped from the group because absentees do not contribute sufficient value to the remaining members.

It's essential that group members understand what other members do because if they don't, they can't make good referrals. To insure such understanding, each member is required to make a one-to-one visit to another member's place of business. Visits usually consist of tours, questions and answers.

During one-to-one visits, the visiting members must give hosts sufficient time to explain what they do, what differentiates them from others in their industry and what is their style or approach with clients. Visiting members much receive sufficient information for them identify opportunities for host and to know where they can implant the host in their contact base. Some members accomplish this in one visit, while others need multiple visits.

One-to-one visits also help members identify problems that their existing clients may be having. Then they can draw from the expertise of the group to solve those problems, which is "networking at the highest level," according to Krauser. "That's our goal."

Once a year, all seven of the Network Associates groups will assemble at a larger venue. Krauser calls this the Network of Networks. Occasionally, he will hold other off site events such as golf outings.

Rules and referrals

Network Associates does not allow members to solicit each other's business and doing so is grounds for automatic expulsion. However, members can approach each other for help or to use each other's services. For example, a mortgage broker can't solicit another other member's business, but the broker can hire the telephone consultant to design a phone system for his/her office.

The group does not permit remuneration between members. So, if you close a deal after receiving a lead from a group member, you can't give them money or even a gift. The only return should be thanks and referrals.

Business between members is inevitable; people do business with those they know, like and trust. All members are entitled to make a profit and can, but are not required to, give other members discounts (but they can if they wish).

Two types of leads are generated in the group: primary and secondary leads or referrals. A primary lead occurs when a group member has a contact and passes it on to another member. For example, when one group member tells another, "Call ABC Industries because they need a new health insurance policy. Speak with Jack Jones and say I told you to call."

A secondary referral is when a member has not been able to hook up with anyone at ABC Industries' or does not have a tight relationship with ABC. At the meeting, that member might ask, "Does anyone have any contacts that could help me at ABC Industries?" Some members may have contacts while others may know someone, say an accountant, who worked with ABC Industries. The member will then give the other member the accountant's name and number, the member will call the accountant and the accountant provides a referral into ABC.

Network Associates' members never count leads; they are not required to give other members a set number of leads. When leads are given, all involved can benefit. If Member A asks Member B to help solve a client's problem, Member A is showing his/her client that he/she is more than his/her core business. And, Member B benefits by receiving a new opportunity.

The group also serves as a resource for its members. When a member, Larry Turell, a life and health insurance whiz, was thinking of refinancing his home so he asked the advice of a mortgage banker who was member of the group. The banker volunteered to talk with Larry, at no charge, and taught Larry the questions to when seeking a mortgage. As a result of the group member's help, Larry was able to get a terrific deal and avoid a lot of the aggravation usually entailed in refinancing.

The meetings

Network Associates has formal business meetings, which Krauser leads.

Between 8 to 8:25 is an informal mixer session, at which members say hello and chat. Coffee and pastries are served. Krauser distributes an agenda and a roster containing the names and contact information of the group members and guests. So, if you're a guest, you don't have to constantly ask, "Who is that?" All you have to do is look at the roster to find who is who.

At 8:25 the formal agenda begins. Krauser starts the formal proceedings by going around the room and asking members to give a five to ten sound bite stating who they are and describing their business. Frequently, Krauser will ask members add to their sound bite by telling the group about their most interesting business experience that month, their most recent business transaction or problems they are encountering in their industry. When Krauser gets to the guests, he asks them to tell the group a little bit more about themselves and exactly what they do.

The next session is called "Getting Down to Business," which generally takes at least an hour. Krauser asks the group, "Does anyone have anything that they're working on that you may need assistance with?" Everyone at the meeting, members and guests, then has the opportunity to state explain what help they need and what project of theirs have problems. The other members may offer, direct help, suggestions or refer the member to someone in their networks who might help.

Throughout the meeting, Krauser makes sure that the members' requests are specific. Some group members often tend to make general statements rather than direct requests. For example, they may state the problem, which group members may not be able to solve. However, if the member asked if anyone had contacts with a certain company, the response could be greater. Krauser questions them to bring out information may trigger help from the others members and guests.

In addition to moderating meetings, Krauser, through his seven groups, has a wide range of contacts. So, he also brings his entire contact base to the meeting as do all the other members and guests present. As a result, some help is usually forthcoming. The real resource is all of these contacts.

The Getting Down to Business segment is the time during the meeting when all of the members have the opportunity to use the entire group.

NETWORKING NUGGET

When Larry Turell's wife Anne's birthday was coming up, he decided to take her to dinner and a Broadway show. To make the occasion more festive, he decided to hire a limo to drive them to and from the Manhattan. Larry wanted the best Limo service, so he called Steve and Steve recommended a service with which he did business. The service was great, they did everything they could to make the evening memorable including arranging for a catering service to deliver a delicious meal that the celebrating couple enjoyed while riding into the City. Not only was the service top notch and non-intrusive, but it gave Larry its preferred customer rate, even though he was a first-time customer, which saved him a bundle.

After the Getting Down to Business segment, a five-minute coffee break follows. During this time, members can follow up on matters raised in the Getting Down to Business portion of the meeting. For example, if two members said they had contacts that could help the lawyer, they would give the lawyer their contacts' information during the break or arrange a subsequent exchange via telephone or email. At this time, further questions can be asked and information exchanged without disturbing or wasting the time of other members.

After the break, Krauser conducts ten to fifteen minutes of networking exercises to help the group polish their networking skills. One exercise, is asking members to list the top five industries that provide them with business. Then he goes around the room and asks two or three members to read off their list. By conducting this exercise, he helps members refocus on whom they should be approaching to get more business. He will also as them to recite their sound bites speeches and critique or help them revise them.

Krauser will also question members on whether they gave to other group members in the last month, whether they got leads back and what kind of leads they were.

The final meeting segment covers two areas: (1) reports on one to one visits and (2) exchanging thanks. Members tell the group about their one-to-one visits and what they learned so others can share their insights about the host's business. Network Associates teaches its members that whenever they make a one-on-one visit, the visitor should give the host a lead. It's a way of saying thanks and of giving, which is so essential in networking. As members learn about the host's operation, they should always think, "Who would be good contact for this member to meet?"

During the final segment, members have the opportunity to thank others for giving them leads in the past month or at this meeting. It's also the time to identify other members whose business you would like to visit. For example, if one member is being thanked often, it shows that the member is doing something right and that that he/she is probably a great candidate for a one-on-one visit.

After the meeting ends, members can hang around to tie up loose ends. They can follow up on information that raised during the meeting, set up one-to-one visits and talk about leads. Members often stay for an additional half hour.

NETWORKING NUGGET

Larry Turell needed a travel agent to book a vacation trip to Europe for him and his wife. Since there was no travel agent in his group, he called Steve for a recommendation. Steve referred Larry to an agent who was a member of one of Steve's other groups. Larry called the agent, they got along well and Larry booked the trip through him. At no cost to Larry, the agent got him round-trip first class tickets. From that point on, the agent got all of Larry's business.

Caterina Rando's Circle of Eight

Business success coach and author Caterina Rando was looking for innovative ways to get better results—faster, and with less energy and resource output. An area that challenged her was how business people could generate qualified leads: find potential clients for their products or services. As a result, she devised a solution that she believes produces more leads and enhances members' careers in less time and for just pennies a day. Rando says her idea is innovative because "It works for anyone, anywhere, on any budget."

The genesis of the Circle of Eight came from the book *The Tipping Point*, in which author Malcolm Gladwell detailed studies that showed that people easily remember seven things. For example, if ten different people who were standing in front of you suddenly vanished, you would easily recall seven of them. Additionally, Rando cites research that found that members of leads-exchange groups usually have seven people with whom they consistently exchange reciprocal leads.

The relatively small size of a Circle of Eight is makes it controllable and not unwieldy. Members can communicate easily, develop closer relationships, learn about each other's businesses and needs and be alert for leads for other Circle members. A Circle of Eight is inexpensive to launch and maintain. You select seven complimentary partners for your Circle and tap into their networks, smarts, experience and resources.

To create a Circle of Eight, identify companies or individuals who provide a different, but complimentary, product or service from what you provide. Also make sure that your Circle members are all seeking the same customer profile. Select members who you trust, like, respect and with whom you will be happy to be identified. Choose carefully because if one or two members don't measure up, the Circle could collapse or, worse yet, your reputation could be tarnished.

Pick compatible partners, who are involved in businesses that will work with your group. For example, an interior designer who specializes in office design might invite into her Circle of Eight an architect, a painting contractor, a office-furniture dealer, an electrical contractor, a floor-covering firm, a landscape architect and a lighting-fixtures company.

In a Circle of Eight, meetings are held via the phone on a conference or bridge line. Forty-five minute sessions are scheduled every two or three weeks to keep connected, ask questions and exchange ideas. Members can network with other members from all over the country without leaving their offices and be the first to learn of regional trends that they could import. Rando assembled eight experts/speakers from different regions throughout the country and Canada for her Circle. In your Circle of Eight, you can partner with firms that are based anywhere instead of being forced to partner with nearby firms of lesser value. You can seek out the best wherever they are located.

As soon as a Circle member comes across a lead, he/she circulates it electronically to all members. This allows Circle members to get leads quickly and act immediately on those that interest them. With seven other people beating the bushes for leads for you, your opportunities will multiply. Since all information is sent directly to your computer, you can easily categorize, calendar and file it, which helps you stay well organized.

A Circle member is selected to be the facilitator for each meeting. When circle members get together by phone for their sessions, they follow a regular agenda. Sessions start with each member giving a quick report on the status of his/her business. Then each member informs the group how many leads, resources or strategic referrals they have given the other members. In the Circle,

- A lead is something that leads to financial remuneration
- A resource is someone or something that can provide help and
- A strategic referral is something that will help a member, but does not involve payment. For example, speaking at an even that does not pay a fee, but will boost the member's career.

During the sessions, members report on how much they made from referrals from the Circle. They also tell the other Circle members how many leads they will provide and how many speeches they will book by the next Circle meeting.

In addition, members discuss projects they have heard about in areas of interest to Circle members. They also find out about other Circle members' needs or interests and areas where they can partner, refer or help. Members can brainstorm ideas, share referrals and connect other members to both current and past clients who might be interested in a Circle member's services. Members can also discuss innovations in their respective industries, which could work for other members.

Members can also provide each other with resources. They can recommend vendors, share cost-cutting and technical innovations and inform other members about trade shows and other upcoming events of interest. Members can also enter into cooperative marketing ventures such as partnering on mailings or ads that would be prohibitively expensive for any one member.

Circles of Eight usually become circles of friends because the members seek and depend upon each other for advice and resources. Each Circle member gains valuable support because the other members serve as his/her sounding boards, Board of Directors, expanded sales force and allies. The key feature of a Circle of Eight is that all members actively search for opportunities that will advance the other members and their businesses.

Consider creating your own Circle of Eight. Rando's blueprint can be adapted to fit diverse situations, is easy to operate and can provide great rewards. Plus, you don't have to mortgage the farm.

The Hubble Group

The Hubbel Group was a loosely-knit, grass roots, women's group that sprung to life in Spokane, Washington, and enjoyed a remarkably productive five-year run. In that time, it enriched many women's lives and profoundly changed the community.

In 1997, Julia Hubbel's world collapsed, she lost her job, lost her land, got divorced and ended up living in a Spokane, Washington, with few friends, contacts or prospects. Plus, health was a serious mess. Desperate for work, she joined every organization, networked like mad and sent out 400 resumes. She got one interview, but not the job. She filed for bankruptcy and lost her house, car, credit rating, career, her dogs and her self-respect … everything but her gumption.

While Hubbel's life was falling apart, the seeds of her networking started to sprout. In her travels, she met wonderful women who were at the top of their fields: entrepreneurs, community leaders, senior regional directors, executive vice presidents, artists, writers, dancers and university professors. Through her networking efforts, she found Spokane to be an insular and conservative community that didn't know what to do with the emergence of so many high-powered women. Hubbel also realized that these women needed to meet each other, form a support group and she could make it happen.

Hubbel scheduled lunch with one of the women and was so impressed that she couldn't wait to introduce her to other women she had been getting to know. The next time they met for lunch, a third woman joined them and "it was overwhelming." By the fourth lunch, nine women showed up, all hand-picked from Hubbel's growing list of friends/contacts. None knew each other, but they instantly liked, respected and realized that they needed each other. So, they agreed to meet regularly.

Within three years, the group grew to 60 members, with a core group of about sixteen who were the most active. In between meetings, Hubbel networked to recruit potential members.

Originally they called themselves the Great Broads, but they became Hubbel Group to appear more professional. Hubbel personally interviewed each new candidate over a cup of coffee to see if she would fit. During interviews, Hubbel tried to spot the woman's needs and connect her to group members who could help, even those women who did not join. Age was not a determinative and members ranged from 27 to 54. The requirements for membership were brains, accomplishments, skills, an understanding of the need to give for the larger good and the need to learn how to receive from other women. The women who joined did so to serve and make a difference. The Hubbel Group never competed with, but complemented, the area's existing women's groups.

The group met for lunch once a month. It charged no dues; the only requirement was that the women show up and be totally present for the 90-minute lunch. At meetings, the women went around the table and answered a set of questions, staying within a crisp time frame in order to give everyone a turn.

At meetings, each woman:

- Told the group what she did better than anyone, without using I think, or I guess, or other wishy-washy language. The sentence had to begin with "I'm the best _____" so the others would know what she had to offer.
- Told the group about a recent event she wanted to celebrate: a contract, a promotion, a political appointment, a job offer, a new grandchild or anything else that she wished to share with the group. At this point, the speaker had her time in the spotlight.
- Told the group about updates or news of interest to the members such as a high-level dinner, a political campaign needing volunteers, a job posting, community news of importance or whatever may have an impact on the group members' lives. Updates brought special value women who traveled or didn't move in the same circles.
- Asked for help from the group. According to Hubbel, this was by far the hardest part. The women asked for advice on potentially difficult legal situations at work, marketing an email list or referrals for a job; it didn't matter. In response, the group enthusiastically jumped in and tithed their social capital. The group members, who were powerful women, competed to brainstorm and put forth the best solutions. At the next meeting, the women who had requested help reported on how the solutions worked.

All of the women spoke up at each meeting, which enhanced their relationships and the quality of the time that they spent together. Instead of racing for the door at the end of meetings, a group of stragglers always remained to talk, which frequently lasted until mid-afternoon.

On the first Friday of each month, the group hosted a regular potluck dinner. The potluck allowed them to spend comfortable for hours at a member's house and further develop their relationships. As they grew closer, they bought from each other, laughed with each other, provoked each other, promoted each other and grew with each other.

Over time, the Hubbel Group provided referrals to local boards and placed a woman on the Chamber of Commerce Board. They mentored young women coming out of the military to help them find high-paying corporate jobs. They supported each other through divorces, job and location changes.

Smaller, more intimate groups grew out of the larger whole as members formed closer bonds with groups of four or five. Those in the offshoot groups, continued to draw on resources within the group, celebrated accomplishments, supported each other through hard or sad times and found different reasons to become active in the community.

In 2000, Julia Hubbel moved to Colorado to be close to her ailing mother. The group found another leader and continued to meet for another eighteen months. Since then, the friendships formed in the group have remained intact, but the group dissolved.

"The most important lesson I learned through The Hubbel Group was that when I believed I had nothing to give, I discovered that I had everything to give. When I had hit rock-bottom and was facing living out of a cardboard box on the street in a city far from family and friends, I found a way to be of service. And through The Hubbel Group I discovered that when everything else is stripped away, all the trappings of power and influence that we believe that are so powerful, all people really want from us is to be acknowledged and valued. By providing that to these powerful women, and by putting them together and helping to foment their relationships through celebration and storytelling, we changed much more than many women's lives. We helped change the face of a community."

AmSpirit Business Connections
(formerly Network Professionals, Inc., Greater Ohio Region)

AmSpirit Business Connections is an organization that assists sales representatives, entrepreneurs and professionals succeed by creating a forum where they can exchange qualified referrals. The focus of AmSpirit is giving to others and enabling members to serve as resources for their customers and clients. In doing so, AmSpirit members have the opportunity to meet other professionals they would not otherwise meet, while improving their business communication skills.

"A qualified referral," is being given the name of a person or firm that will be expecting your call. The object is for members to put one another in touch with legitimate business opportunities that will further their careers.

As we go to press, AmSpirit has over 50 chapters, but is engaged in a dynamic expansion program that is expected to add at least 20 chapters annually. As a result, it is seeking entrepreneurial-minded individuals who to serve as organization directors.

The logistics

Chapters vary in size and average about 15 members per chapter and include both men and women. They meet weekly for regularly scheduled morning meetings, for example from 7:30 AM to 8:45 on every Thursday. Chapters meet in a wide variety of public meeting spaces. Members have one-on-one luncheon meetings once a month and periodic social events. Chapters also have Web sites and publish monthly newsletters.

Only one member from a business category can belong to a chapter. Therefore, for example, a chapter can have only one landscaper, one jeweler and one dentist. To join AmSpirit applicants pay a $210 initiation fee and quarterly membership dues of $60. If the four quarterly membership payments are paid at one time, members get a discount and pay only $215.

Members usually network other people into the organization. For instance, an attorney may recruit and accountant, who will recruit a financial consultant, who will bring in a mortgage broker and so on.

The members of each chapter have the right to determine who will be accepted for membership. When applicants are rejected, it's usually because the members felt that their category was not sufficiently beneficial to the chapter. For example, the members of a professionally-oriented chapter may reject a hair stylist on the ground that he/she would not make a strong enough contribution to their group. Chapters may reject applicants for other reasons including the fact that a member had an unpleasant experience with an applicant, the applicant has a bad reputation or simply on the basis of personalities.

Meetings

Some chapters send out agendas prior to meetings or post them on their Web sites. AmSpirit has structured meetings that all chapters basically follow. However, the speakers at each chapter change from meeting to meeting.

When members arrive at meetings, they are encouraged to greet everyone and shake hands. In one chapter, members can be fined $25 for not shaking hands. The members then have coffee, mingle and network.

The president, who is chosen by chapter members, kicks off each meeting by asking another member to read the chapter's charter. The charter sets forth the purpose of the organization; reading it focuses the members focused and gives guests an overall understanding of the organization's objectives. The president then asks members who have brought guests to introduce the guests. The guests have the opportunity to stand up, tell the group what they do and explain how the group can help them. Guests usually speak for two to three minutes.

Chapter officers then report on developments in their area. For example, the officer in charge of scheduling the chapter's programs will announce the list of speakers for the next few meetings.

After the officers report, the chapter program begins. Each week, a chapter member will give a presentation about his/her business. In the presentation, the member will describe the benefits his/her business provides and tell chapter members what they need.

In most chapters, the presentations last for about 20 minutes, but others schedule two speakers for 10 minutes each. AmSpirit chapters do not use outside speakers. Occasionally, a chapter may decide not to have a speaker and the central AmSpirit organization will provide them with training materials on networking or the central organization's staff will visit to conduct networking training.

After the chapter program, new members will be introduced, given membership certificates and final announcements will be made. All of the members will then give a short introduction; talk briefly about their business and their needs and make referrals. If they received referrals from people at the meeting, they will thank and update them about the referrals.

Central organization

The central AmSpirit organization operates under the philosophy that the chapters belong to the members. Therefore, it exercises a loose control over the chapters in terms of the meeting contents and lets each chapter develop its unique character. The central organization takes the position that its role is to serve as (1) a guide to help the chapters implement the organization's structure and (2) a team of coaches who share with the chapters its experience on what it believes will and will not work.

AmSpirit maintains and information-based Web site to enhance communications and the dissemination of information within the organization. Electronic networking forums are available on the Web site for the posting of information and messages. The forums are intended to increase communications between members. Postings are related to general matters involving networking and events such as socials, joint meetings, new chapter information, conferences, etc. Messages on the forums can be commercial in nature, but cannot directly solicit referrals for members' businesses.

Operating philosophies

"There is a formula behind networking. It's like being healthy. We know what it takes to be healthy: drink eight glasses of water each day, exercise and eat a balance diet and chances are you'll be healthy. The formula for networking is that you give referrals; you get to know, like and trust people in your network; let them get to know, like and trust you and give a concise, clear message as to who you are and what you do. This is what we teach. If you do these things, you raise the likelihood of your success tenfold," according to AmSpirit's Founder and CEO, Frank Agin.

Rules

Members are required to regularly attend meetings; they are expected to attend three out of four meetings each month. If a member does not satisfy the attendance requirement, the chapter has the right "to open up the category," which means to drop the member from the chapter and bring in someone from the same category, such as a real estate broker, an accountant or a financial planner.

AmSpirit members are asked to give at least two qualified referrals each month, which is seldom a problem. Those who don't give qualified referrals, generally end up dropping out. Either of the two expected monthly qualified referrals may be given to members of other AmSpirit chapters.

NETWORKING NUGGET

"The great networking stories are those of people who join the organization and slug away and persevere at building relationships," Agin explained. "Not the quick successes. A realtor in one of our chapters has been in the organization for ten years. For the first two years, he didn't get a single referral, but he stuck with it, built relationships and did what needed to be done. Since that initial drought, he has sold upwards of 200 homes because of referrals he received directly through the organization."

Members are encouraged do business with one another. If you don't have a travel agent, you are encouraged to use one who is in your chapter or another AmSpirit chapter. Soliciting other members is frowned upon and difficult to police. As a result, members quietly solicit business. Members tend to join the organization because they don't like the typical sales approach, so aggressive solicitations are rare and usually backfire.

Referral fees are not prohibited, but they are not encouraged. The organization is founded on the premise that members should give without expectation and the practice of giving referral fees creates expectations. However, an exception exists in the case of large corporations that have a referral fee program in place. In those instances, receiving referral fees are acceptable. Most members refer clients to other members because they trust the other member to serve their client well, which makes the referring member look good to his/her client. When referral fees are given, it also could raise the question of whether a referrer's primary motive in referring a client was to serve the client or to cash in on a referral fee.

eWomenNetwork

eWomenNetwork, Inc.(eWN), is an organization headquartered in Dallas, Texas that connects female business owners and professionals with one another. It supports, promotes and showcases its members' products and services and helps them achieve their professional objectives. eWomenNetwork teaches that networking is the art of giving and searching for ways to serve the needs of others before focusing on yourself. It instructs members to be "other-focused."

The organization bills itself as "the #1 resource for connecting and promoting women and their businesses worldwide." It also claims to be the "fastest growing membership-based professional women's networking organization in North America. "We are the marketing machine for women owned businesses and corporate professionals," eWN cofounder and CEO Sandra Yancy stated. "Every initiative we take on must answer the question, "Does it connect women and does it promote them?"

Membership

eWN has over 100 chapters across North America and is rapidly expanding. Members join the national organization, not merely the local chapters, so they can attend meetings or events at any eWomenNetwork venue. Both individual and corporate memberships are offered.

An applicant pays a one-time, life-time $290 initiation fee. She then pays $16.95 per month for membership benefits, which includes having her business profiled on the eWomenNetwork.com Web site and having a link created from eWomenNetwork.com to her personal or business Web site. Under its Three For Free program, the initiation fee will be refunded if a member, at any time during the term of her membership, recommends three new members who are profiled on the Web site. "We are powerful visual connectors," Robin Ramsey, eWN's Managing Director for San Francisco noted. "So we want to make sure that members don't simply register their membership, but we also want them to put their profiles up on our Web site."

In addition to maintaining members' Web site profiles, members receive discounts at the organization's Accelerated Networking Events (ANEs), which is the term eWN uses for chapter meetings. Members are also entitled to receive discounts for conferences and for the products of companies that have strategic alliances allied with eWN.

With their membership, women get two complimentary coaching sessions from eWN's Premier Success Coaches, who are all certified and experienced coaches. Coaches specialize in a number of areas such as coaching for moms, coaching for creativity and coaching from the legal perspective, which is provided by an attorney. "Success doesn't happen by accident. It is planned, it's intentional," Yancy stresses. "The coaching benefit allows members to be totally self-absorbed and selfish for a couple hours where the focus is only on them and their business. When you are intentional and plan for your success, all of the other things fall into better order." Members also have access to eWN's premier faculty, which is composed of noted authors and experts in a number of diverse fields.

Business platform

eWN has a six pronged business platform. All of the components are well in place except the television programming, which as we went to press was still under development. The six parts of the business platform are WomenNetwork's:

- Web site
- Face-to-face networking
- Radio programming
- Print publications
- Nonprofit foundation
- Television programming

The Web site

eWomenNetwork.com has the world's largest photographic database of women entrepreneurs and women professionals. It gets 3 million hits per month. "Our members go on it all the time," says Yancy. "Which tells us that it's working." The site contains profiles of eWN's members and their contact information. Members can post three graphic images with their profile and the eWN database is searchable by names, business categories and geographical areas. The site also includes the members' forum, the last four eWomenNetwork. com radio shows, testimonials, listing of affiliate alliances as well as photos and information on its managing directors (chapter leaders), premier coaches and premier faculty. A special offers page lists organizations that give discounts to eWN members and an events calendar page provides a map showing where events around the country will be held.

Members can network through the members' forum, which allows them to promote their businesses, offer specials or simply ask questions.

NETWORKING NUGGET

Sandra Yancy needed an engraver in the Dallas area. The eWomenNetwork International Conference was fast approaching and the organization would be presenting a lot of gifts that needed to be engraved. She checked the eWN membership, but couldn't locate a member who was a local engraver, so she went to the forum. Yancy posted a request for referrals to an engraver in the Dallas area and within 48 hours, she had eleven recommendations. From these recommendations, Yancy found her engraver, who did a wonderful job. "That's the beauty of online networking!" Yancy exclaimed.

Face-to-face networking

An Accelerated Networking Events (chapter meetings) take place at each of the 75 chapters across North America once each month. ANEs are conducted by a managing director. To be a managing director, a woman must have corporate experience or have owned her own business. She must believe that networking is a key component to being successful and the concept that networking is about giving and not about getting. ANEs are run according to eWN's guidelines and every chapter follows the same basic format. The organization has few rules and feels that the type of members it attracts does require formalized standards.

ANEs are either luncheon events or late afternoon/evening receptions and last for two hours. Display tables are available for women to promote their products or services. Members are encouraged to arrive no later than one-half hour before the meeting is scheduled so that they can network informally. The cost to attend an ANE varies with each chapter, but the average is $35 for members, $48 for nonmembers and $55 for those (both members or guests) who do not sign up until five days before the event. Guests can attend two ANEs, but if they wish to attend more, they must become eWN members.

ANEs are held at hotels, restaurants or private clubs. Upon entering, the women are given name tags and they select a place to sit. Members are encouraged not to sit with friends and associates and to sit with strangers so they can make new contacts. The ANE program begins with a welcome from the managing director. She briefs the groups on the background of eWN cofounders Sandra and Kym Yancy so that they understand that the organization is operated by accomplished and highly successful business professionals. Members and display table sponsors are introduced and a short video is shown that explains the eWN vision and describes the organization. Then structured networking rounds begin.

In round one, each woman is given a card with a number from one to eight. She is told to get up from her seat, all the other women who have the same number and sit with them in a circle. In the circles, each woman states who she is, what service or product she provides and what she wants in the next 30 days. She is given two minutes to state this information. Members are encouraged to identify who they know that could help other members. If a woman in the group can help, she hands the other woman her business card with a notation written on it. Exchanging blank cards is not permitted. Therefore, if Woman A wrote "Bob" on the back of the card she gave Woman

B, when Woman B calls, she will remind Woman A that she wrote that "Bob" on her card. This will focus their conversation and build on the rapport they developed at the ANE. "Men do business based on reports, women do business based on rapport," Ramsey declared.

According to Yancy, ANEs teach women "how to condense their interactions because women get caught up in the connecting piece of it. They get involved in saying, 'Hi, how are you, how did you get into the business, Do you live here? How long have you been here? Do you have kids, what school do they go to?' etc. It's great because it plants seeds in our brains for later recollections of someone, but it can also prevent us from moving from that interaction, to what I call 'transaction.' The point is to get women to get down to the business of business."

The women then return to their original seats and the managing director gives them statistics about women in the business world. She also inquires about round one and how it went, if they got leads or made valuable contacts. Lunch, which was placed on the tables while the women were in the circles, now begins. The managing director then introduces the speaker who speaks for 20 minutes.

After lunch, the women get up and move to another area for round two. In round two, they sit with the other women from their table. In round two, each woman again states who she is, what her product or service is and what she wants in the next 30 days. They then return to the table and the managing director reviews round two and inquires how it went.

The final ANE segment is the raffle, which is designed to familiarize the group with the members' products or services. "We always hear women say, 'If people would try my products, I know they would like and buy them,'" Yancy reports. "So, we raffle their products and services to provide that chance." Members donate their products or services and the other women at the ANE buy raffle tickets. Tickets are $1 each or 8 for $5. The winners can use the products and services, endorse them, continue to purchase and use them or refer them to others. Proceeds from the raffles are donated to the eWomenNetwork Foundation, which allocates the funds to other nonprofit groups in the region where the monies were received.

Radio programming

The eWomenNetwork Radio show is broadcast live every Sunday from 7 to 8 PM, central time. It is carried on the number one ABC affiliate in the nation and penetrates 80 percent of the country. Plus, the programs can be heard live on the Internet.

The purpose of the radio show, which is hosted by Sandra Yancy, is to spotlight eWN members and to create greater awareness of them. Subjects post their profiles and are interviewed by Sandra. The programs are not infomercials, but are conversational. Questions usually asked include, "What are your challenges?" "Why did you do this?" "What is going on with you now?" "How are you surviving these times?" "What's the greatest success that you have?" "What do you need?" and "How can our listeners connect with you?"

The four most recent radio programs are archived at eWomenNetwork. com. If a member who is listening wants to contact any of the women profiled, she can look her up on the database on the Web site, which contains her target's contact information.

Print publications

eWN has affiliate alliances and cross promotes with women's publications across the nation. These publications run ongoing ads for the eWomenNetwork and publish articles and information about the organization and its members. In turn, eWN promotes the publications to its members. Through its print alliances, eWN informs the public about its activities and achievements, attracts new members and gets wide publicity for itself and its members.

Nonprofit eWomenNetwork Foundation

The nonprofit eWomenNetwork Foundation helps women in need, "those who have it really tough." It also conducts a "fementoring" program for young women in high school and college. The purpose of the foundation is to nurture and grow up-and-coming women who will become the business leaders tomorrow. The foundation contributes to and supports other nonprofit corporations that focus on helping women in need and is conducting a pilot intern program, under which interns will receive college credit. eWN will be encouraging the establishment of similar intern programs in its chapters.

"The eWomenNetwork Foundation is as important an artery to the heart of the organization as the other components. I believe morally that what we are doing is about leaving this planet a better place and most importantly leaving it a better road for women," Yancy explained.

Conferences and events

In addition to its other activities, eWN also runs several major events. Among them are its annual international conference, which usually lasts four days, a holiday extravaganza that is generally held the first Thursday of each December and one-day Business Exchanges and Expos at the chapters. Sandra Yancy and/or a nationally-recognized speaker will frequently appear at the Business Exchanges and Expos.

✫✫✫ Action steps ✫✫✫

1. List the five organized groups in your area where you could best network.

_____

_____

_____

_____

_____

2. State your three major objectives in joining organized networking groups.

_____

_____

3. Set forth the features or organized networking groups that appeal to you.

_____

_____

4. List features of organized networking groups that you wish to avoid.

_____

_____

CHAPTER 9

EVALUATING NETWORKING GROUPS AND EVENTS

*"The success of each is dependent
of the success of the other."*
—John D. Rockefeller, Jr.

This chapter will cover:
- ❏ *Complicating factors*
- ❏ *The selection process*
- ❏ *Return on investment*
- ❏ *Seminal questions*
- ❏ *Maintaining the connection*
- ❏ *Subsequent benefits*
- ❏ *Review productivity*

The number of networking groups and networking events to choose from is overwhelming. Each is unique and promises to deliver special benefits that you can't possibly live without. Joining and attending all of them is impossible and even it you could join them all, it would bankrupt you. So you must be extremely selective.

Unfortunately, being selective isn't so easy. It's a complicated process that takes more than simply signing up with a group recommended by your most trusted buddies or the first group or event that appeals to you. A number of underlying factors complicate the evaluation process. They are as follows:

- As a rule, the benefits of networking groups increase in direct proportion to the regularity of your attendance. Maximum benefits usually flow when you become a fixture at group meetings and events. If you're always there, you become a part of the in-group, the inner circle. You become privy the inner workings of the organization and its future plans. When you're in the inner circle, people will think of you when they think about the group or its events. As a regular attendee, you can meet and build closer relationships with key organization members and nonmembers who come in contact with the group. Usually, your prominence in the organization increases with length and the degree of your involvement, as does your visibility. If you attend only every other meeting, chances are that you will reap fewer and less meaningful benefits than if you attend every meeting. If you drop by occasionally, expect occasional benefits.

- Networking groups are always in flux. Members come and go or attend irregularly, which changes the organization's dynamic. As a result, the leadership and the group's agenda also change. In addition, the objectives of groups can also shift with the success or failure of how the group's projects and events are received. While an influx of new members can breathe life into a static, old group and get it moving in exciting, new directions, it can cast faithful, established members off to the side and out of the loop. Features that initially drew you to the group may no longer exist and it may feel like you belong to a different group than the one you thought you joined. Like people, organizations also bog down, become stale, tired and dated. Causes that were once vital and compelling are eclipsed by new and more pressing concerns, which may not interest or serve you. Overall, organizations can be of varying value to you at different times and it's hard to predict when those times will occur.

- You can't spread yourself too thin. If you try to attend too many group meetings and events, you'll give few, if any, the time and attention they deserve. Most likely, you'll end up wasting your valuable time and money. In addition, it will be physically exhausting and the energy you need for other endeavors will be sapped. It makes no sense to sign up and pay for an event and then sleep or sleep walk through the most important presentations. Finally, by spreading yourself so thinly, other group members might feel alienated if they get the impression that you're not giving their pet group or event your full effort and attention.

- Finally, those who recommend groups and events, may have different agendas than you. They may be involved in a group to increase their business while you want to serve your community; they may want publicity while you want anonymity; they may want to socialize and get dates, while you may not be in the market. In addition, group members often work to enlist new blood to increase their own clout within the organization. They may fudge when they describe what you're about to get into and when you join, you may find yourself smack-dab in the middle of a political brawl. Finally, groups that your best pals truly love may not be the best fit for you or the best use of your resources.

The selection process

Most people select networking groups and events by identifying a few contenders and trying each out. If they like a group and it seems productive, they stick with it and if not, they don't join. However, as we have said, groups constantly change and you must participate for a time before the maximum benefits kick in.

A better approach is researching each prospective networking group or event before you join or attend. Identify, and in the space below, list the reasons why each group or event is attractive to you. Then list your objectives and be specific. Ask yourself who do you want to meet? Name the precise people or categories of people. Do you want to meet others in your field, business people from other industries or do you want to join groups that provide services and help in the community? What do you expect get from each event?

Consider whether the groups and events that interest you will be convenient or whether they will disrupt other important parts of you life. Are they held at places you can easily reach and at times that you can make? Will you have to rearrange your life in order to attend and if so, is it worth it to you? Are there more convenient alternatives? Convenience is important. Don't obligate yourself to attend a meeting or event that could end up being more trouble than its worth because, in time, you'll probably stop attending.

In making your selections, also don't discount the enjoyment factor. People who have fun network better. Spending time enjoyably adds to the quality of your life, it makes you anticipate, feel enthusiastic about and look forward to upcoming meetings and events. People who are happy tend to be more relaxed, approachable and attractive to others. They also prefer to be around happy people as opposed to grumps, don't you? If you enjoy the groups and events you attend, you will probably be more enthusiastic, which will enable you to communicate your desires with more passion.

Usually, the first consideration in the selection process is identifying whom you can meet. Select your targets. If you want to meet people in your industry, think about trade and industry associations. For example, if you're a lawyer, it makes sense to join the bar association; if you're a female entrepreneur, consider the National Association of Women Business Owners and if you're a graphic designer, try the American Institute of Graphic Arts.

At meetings and events sponsored by trade and industry associations, you can meet your peers; discuss common problems such as recent changes in the industry and even develop working or referral arrangements. You can serve on committees that can increase your visibility within your business, industry and community. With greater visibility, you can meet and work with the policy and decision makers and extend your network to the higher echelons of your field.

If you want to meet people who are in different businesses, try business-oriented groups such as the Chamber of Commerce, eWomenNetwork, CEO Space or AmSpirit Business Connections. These organizations cater to people from a wide mix of businesses. If you have a product or service that would fit well with another industry, think about joining organizations or attending events directed at that industry where you can cross-market. For example, an ambitious flower arranger should consider attending meetings of associations for wedding planners, funeral directors and event organizers. If you want to establish a strong community base, think about joining service groups, community, civic or religious groups.

After you've identified the networking groups or events that might work for you, ask the members of your network for their opinions before you sign up. Learn if they have attended the group's meetings or events and if not, do they know others who have. When you connect with others who have attended groups and events, ask them for a descriptive overview. Pay close attention to what they describe first and the level of their enthusiasm. Then zero in on the details: how many people attend, where the group met, how it was organized, how long meetings ran, did they follow a formal agenda, what items were on the agenda and what was the tone of the meeting? Was it lighthearted, all business, formal, casual or competitive? Did many people participate or did a few hog the floor? Was there a mixer of social component and if so, when did it take place and were the members or attendees accessible, warm and friendly?

As we previously stressed, the objectives those you question may differ from your interests. So factor their objectives in before making your decision.

Return on investment

In selecting which groups to join or events to attend, analyze whether it is a smart investment of your time and resources. Hellen Davis, President of Indaba Training Specialists, Inc., and author of the *21 Laws of Influence,* is one of the most successful networkers we know. She graciously contributed the following gems when we interviewed her for this book.

Davis says, "I only attend organized networking events if I can anticipate a 500% return on my investment (ROI)—for the cost of the event and most importantly—for my time. I learned early in business that networking events can be expensive, especially when you're first starting in business or are on a limited budget. And I learned that the cost of the event has to be factored in as ROI", Davis said. "If you're weighing whether to go to one event that costs $50 or another that is $250, determine which should return a better ROI. Just because an event is inexpensive doesn't mean that you will get a better ROI. It might be more advisable to spend the extra money and attend the more expensive event rather than two or three less costly networking affairs.

Hard costs

Hard costs are your purchases. What type of hard costs should you factor in? In calculating hard costs, include the price of admission, parking fees and transportation expenses such as gas, vehicle and maintenance expenses. In addition, to get the most out of events, you must well prepared. So purchase all business materials that are appropriate to properly prepare you for the event. Calculate all of the above expenditures as hard costs.

Soft costs

Soft costs are the opportunity costs and the cost of your time. Focus on the soft costs by asking the following questions:

- Is attending this event the best use of your time?
- Who do you hope to meet?
- Do you have a realistic expectation of doing business over either the short or long term?

If you earn $500 per day and will have to spend four hours at the event, your return from attending the event should be—at the very least—$1,250, plus the recovery of your hard costs.

Calculation

At $500 per day, four hours of your time is worth $250.
$250 x 500% yields a ROI factor of $1,250.

If you plan to stay in business, be realistic and select the events you decide to attend by calculating the anticipated ROI. Ask yourself, "Is this the best use of my time? Can I get a better ROI if I spend my time networking elsewhere?"

Seminal questions

Before you sign up for a networking event, there are several questions you must answer. They are:

- Whom do I expect to meet at the event?
- Will someone on my Top 100 Prospecting List going be in attendance?
- If so, will I have the opportunity to meet him/her?

The opportunity to meet someone high on your Prospecting List can reason enough to attend event. If you've got the right names on your targeted Prospecting List, contacting one of them can return more than a 500% ROI. To calculate the soft cost, ask the following questions:

- What would it cost in time and effort to try to meet that individual?
- How realistic would my chances of meeting him/her be?
- Would we have to be on the same charitable board to meet?
- Will that ever happen?
- Are there less expensive and more beneficial ways to meet this person?
- If so, what are they?

A client of Davis's told her she was going to a book signing to meet and hopefully do business with a certain celebrity. Davis asked her client, "Can you meet the celebrity any other way? She pointed out that the celebrity might not appreciate being pitched at a book signing and that it could do her client more harm than good to approach the celeb at an inappropriate time and place. Then she asked, "How much time would it take to get in the door another way? Who do you know who knows the celebrity or their gatekeepers – agent, TV station, director, author, etc. Would you ever get the opportunity to meet them if I did not attend this event?"

As it worked out, the local ABC affiliate was the first station where the celebrity worked. Davis' client knew the news director who knew the station manager. Two months later the celebrity and Davis' client met for lunch in New York City, which was certainly better than a pitch than at a book signing! Since that lunch they've built and maintained a strong relationship.

NETWORKING NUGGET

In 1996, Davis was invited to attend an event sponsored by the Republican Party in Philadelphia. The event was held at Hope's Cookies, an up-and-coming female-owned business, and was organized to attract more women to the GOP and to show the media that the Republican Party was female-friendly. To do so, the event organizers pulled together twenty of Pennsylvania's top female entrepreneurs to meet Senator Robert Dole, who was then running for the presidency.

Just before the program began, Davis found herself standing with a group of women at the rear of the hall because the front rows were occupied exclusively by men ... the GOP elite. When Hellen joked about the irony of this arrangement to the women standing with her, they began laughing uproariously. As more and men were escorted to front-row seats, the women could barely contain themselves and began laughing hysterically.

When an event organizer rushed over to restore decorum, Davis let him in on the joke. The organizer turned crimson, rushed to the front of the hall, evicted the men and replaced them with Davis and the female standees. Later in the program, when Senator Dole appeared, he immediately commented on how wonderful it was to see so many women in attendance.

During a break, the CEO of the area's largest water company complimented Davis on her initiative in getting a front and center seat and asked how she did it. He laughed at the story they chatted pleasantly until the program resumed. When the program was completed, the event organizer thanked Davis for saving his job and the water company executive suggested that he get Davis on the news since she had saved him. They laughed and agreed to meet for lunch the following week. Shortly thereafter, the organizer introduced Davis to a producer for Dateline who was there with a film crew from the local network affiliate, to cover the event. They interviewed Davis for Dateline and the local news.

That evening, Davis' interview ran locally, but her Dateline spot was cut. The next day two clients called Davis to tell her that they saw her interview. One mentioned that he had not realized that she was a Republican and was considered one of the area's top businesswomen. He wanted to make sure that his company expanded its support for Indaba and he helped set up a meeting for the following week through which Indaba landed a substantial contract.

The other client called and confirmed that Indaba was on the short-list of companies earmarked to provide sales training for their medical representatives in three countries. He said that he had just informed the company President that he had seen Davis on the news clip on the Dole function. Two days later, he called again and told Davis that the contract was hers. Oh, and by the way, could she let them know when the Senator was expected back in town? Davis quickly called the still-beholden event organizer, got and relayed the information to her client. Within ten minutes, her client was "in-the-know" and thankful to be able to be able to provide his boss with timely information.

When she lunched with the water company CEO, Davis explained her business and the types of companies she sought as clients. As it happened, the CEO was on the Board of a large insurance company, he referred Davis to the company's CEO and Davis easily obtained an appointment. At the meeting, the insurance executive arranged for Davis to meet his executive team to pave the way for Indaba to provide training for its field representatives. An executives at that meeting suggested that Davis meet the Director of Human Resources, which resulted in Indaba's putting together a program to train all of the company's home office employees for the next few years. Indaba still provides that service.

Subsequently, three of the company's executives went on to work for other corporations. All of these new companies hired Davis and Indaba to provide consulting, executive coaching, and/or training.

Maintaining the connection

Davis understands that networking is about keeping in touch with people you meet and find interesting. So she maintains an extensive system in which she records their contact information and keeps current on their likes and dislikes – on both a business and personal level.

Keeping up on her contacts helped Davis reap rewards from the Republican event. Every once in a while, she would pop an email off to the Dateline producer and eventually they became friends and traded jokes. On several occasions, Davis hooked the producer up with experts and speakers even though she knew that she would not directly benefit. She helped the producer in order to keep the communication channels open.

Two years after the Republican event, a newsworthy story came to light that Davis thought Dateline might be interested in airing. So she called the producer. Because of the relationship they had established, the producer immediately returned her call. The next week, Davis was interviewed on Dateline and this interview ran. Immediately after it ran, CNN, Extra, Philly After Midnight, and many other radio and TV stations called and interviewed her. Davis calculates that she received over $400,000 worth of free airtime through her Dateline and local appearances and attributes it all to her maintaining contact with the producer.

Davis has also calculated what the original meeting at the Republican event produced. To date, in less than ten years, Indaba has received over $3 million in contracts and media exposure as a direct result of Davis' ability to network from that meeting. Davis continues to meet with the water company's CEO on a regular basis. Whenever they meet, she brings him up to date on the latest branch of the referral tree that they first planted back in 1996. The CEO loves to hear about the people Davis has met through that one event and through his contacts. And guess what? He keeps referring her to his business associates!

Review productivity

Since groups change, as do your needs, review the productivity of the groups and events you attend. After you've been in a group for three months, review whether your membership has been fruitful. If it was, try to calculate the precise financial return to date and prospective future revenues.

If you decide to remain in the organization, review whether it is still worth you time and resources on a regular basis, but at least every three months. Habits form easily. Warm friendships you make with certain group members can keep you involved in groups that no longer provide more essential benefits.

Ask yourself:

- Are your group memberships still productive?
- Are you getting enough of a return to justify your membership?
- Is it a good investment of time, money and energy?

If you are not seeing sufficient returns, it may be time to reassess or rotate your membership. By rotating you can continue as an organization member, but concentrate your focus elsewhere.

Examine whether the Medical Association annual dinner, the Elks Club picnic or your service club's outing were worth you time and money. Again, don't minimize the enjoyment factor, especially with events. If you find that you truly enjoy certain groups or events, don't be too quick to deprive yourself of that pleasure. Work continues and having outlets that you enjoy can yield benefits that may now be hard to envision. So, treat yourself, give yourself the right to have fun and let the network magic work.

★★★ Action steps ★★★

1. *Identify the categories of people that you would like to meet at groups or event.*

_____

_____

_____

2. *Are your group memberships still productive? If so, list why they are productive. If not, list why they are not productive.*

_____

_____

_____

3. *List three groups or events and the return on investment of each.*

_____

_____

_____

4. *List five additional groups or events to investigate joining or attending.*

_____

_____

_____

CHAPTER 10

FOLLOWING UP

"You can be the master of working a room and leave each networking event with a pocketful of business cards, but if you do not follow up with these people and others already in your network, you will never be successful at networking."
—**Andrea Nierenberg**, Author

This chapter will cover:
- ❑ *Business cards*
- ❑ *Utilize a system*
- ❑ *Prioritize*
- ❑ *Make your move*
- ❑ *Always say "thanks"*
- ❑ *Negative responses*
- ❑ *How to follow up*
- ❑ *Follow-up log*

After you've made an interesting new contact who you would like to know better, who could help your career or other aspects of your life, follow up, follow up, follow up. All of the work that you've done to make and impress contacts could be lost if you don't systematically follow up.

Do you know how to follow up? Do you know what to do after you made the first contact? How do you build upon your initial encounter?

Lets hope that when you met your new contact, you followed our suggestions and rattled off that killer sound bite. Hopefully, it impressed your contact and elicited further interest. If it did, did you chat, exchange business cards or contact information? Did you make a date or clearly state that you would like to get together or keep in touch? If you did, great! That's a start, but it's only a start, it's just the tip of the iceberg.

When you make new contacts, you're just getting you foot in the door. Once you have that initial opening, the object is to get in deeper, to get past the gatekeeper and move all the way to the Oval Office. For some people, making initial contacts comes easy; it's an instinctive part of their nature. In most cases, these contacts are brief, little more than introductions that won't go further. However, on occasion, you will want to turn first encounters into more solid relationships, which takes far more time and effort. The bulk of what it takes is following up.

For many, following up is uncomfortable. They usually find it uncomfortable because they don't know what to do. Few of us have ever been taught to network and for many it doesn't come naturally ... at least, that's what we feel. Ironically, when most of us were kids, it was easy to enter into new relationships. We would meet a new kid and see him/her the next day at school, at Little League or at dance class. If we had to call a new kid, it got a little stickier, but generally it was no big deal because most everybody was eager to make new friends. But when we became adults, everything changed.

In our interview, David Hancock said, "Following up starts with being disciplined about the tasks at hand. I am keenly aware that every time I write a task on my daily calendar I am making a promise to myself. I keep those promises knowing that the achievement of my goals will be more than an adequate reward for my discipline. I find it easy to be disciplined, because of the payback offered by the leisure that follows.

"To optimize the process, I stay well organized at home and at work. I do not waste valuable time looking for items that have been misplaced and

I stay organized as I work and as new work comes to me. My astute sense of order is fueled by the efficiency that results from it. I share my ability to organize with those who work with me. Yet, I never squander precious time by becoming over organized. You've never seen follow-up done the way I do it. I stay in touch *constantly* with my prospects. It's not as if I am working at my business, but rather demonstrating *passion* for my work. My goal is to express that passion with excellence and transform it into profits."

Most adults find it hard to follow up. Some are shy, afraid to be a nuisance or to appear to be groveling. The majority; however, simply feel awkward and ill at ease. To them it's unnatural. They see networking as selling and although all of us sell something, they don't want to be perceived as sales persons. Well, if you feel that way, get over it because it's probably holding you back.

> Following up promptly is good business; it's smart business. Following up is as important as any other business task, but most people don't approach it systematically. They think that it should be easy, like when they were kids, and they justify not following up because they are so busy or it's not their style. As a result, they follow up only when they can steal time from other tasks that they consider more important or in desperate attempts to breathe new life into efforts that no longer have life.

In the beginning, following up may feel strange; it may even feel unpleasant, but you'll soon adjust to it. It won't take long, but it will take some time and work and it helps to have a plan. The big surprise is that following up can be fun and it can produce rewards beyond your expectations. It can enable you to meet and form relationships with wonderful people who become close friends and enrich your life.

Utilize a system

Save business cards, contact information and other contact literature. Treat them like receipts that you might need for an IRS audit. Keep all of the original information you collect in a designated place and hold on to it even after you have entered all of the contact information in your files.

Develop a system and follow up religiously in a business-like manner. After making a contact, don't just go home and toss your contract's business card in with the pile of others you collected over the last six months. Business cards won't follow up by themselves. They won't go to the phone, call contacts and make dates for lunch. But you should if you're serious about networking!

Buy or create a system to prioritize and file contact information. Use your mobile device or any of the excellent contact-management software on the market. Many contact-management programs are readily available and most are easy to set up and use. More feature-rich CRM (Contact Relationship Management) systems are also available and the newer systems often include an integrated business card scanner to make the process of entering your new contacts quick and easy. Many CRM systems are setup so that more than one user can access the contacts so that you can assign an assistant or associate for an initial follow up process. Whatever you choose should contain room for your contact's:

- Name
- Business/employer
- Street address
- Email Address
- Telephone number
- Back up telephone numbers including cellular phone numbers
- Fax number
- Web site address
- Specialty area and
- Family information

Also record:

- The names of common friends or contacts
- Source information on how and where you got your contact's name

- Background and personal information such as your contact's education, interests, accomplishments, awards, likes, dislikes, political affiliations, religious affiliations, charitable work and stories or jokes he/she told
- Dates you last spoke and what was said
- Your next step and
- Future plans or actions

Prioritize

Ideally, it's best to enter contact information in your files as close to the initial meeting as possible. Record it that evening or the first thing the next day. Then communicate with your contact via email or postal mail within two or three days to follow up. Unfortunately, most mere mortals are not that organized, disciplined or efficient. We tend to throw all the contact information we collect into a heap and get to it when we get to it ... which won't do!

If you've collected a bunch of business cards, prioritize them to determine who you want to call first. Then enter the contact information into your system. Move first to communicate with:

1. Those you promised to call or email. Place the business cards for those you agreed to contact in a separate stack. Then enter their contact information in your files. Make sure to email or call them within the two or three days of your initial contact. By communicating promptly, you demonstrate that you are a person of your word who does what he/she promised and a person of action. Following up promptly also allows you to build upon the warmth or excitement generated by your exchange or the spirit and fond memories of the event.

2. Contacts who could be important to you. Record his/her contact information in your files immediately. Communicate with him/her within a few days, but no later than a week after you met. Most people are flattered when you call them promptly, especially if the

initial contact was strong. If you made a good connection, contacts will usually be usually delighted to hear from you and be eager to pick off where you left. Calling promptly will not make you seem desperate or uncool. Besides, it's childish, and often self-defeating, to try to be cool with people who could matter.

Call soon. After a week or two, memories get buried by the demands of fast-paced, busy lives … even when you made the most terrific impression. After two or more weeks, consider yourself lucky to be remembered at all.

Classify the business cards you collect in three categories, the:

- A List. Those whom you promised to call and most want to court. Also include those you should thank.
- B List. Contacts you would like to spend time with again or help, but not immediately and
- C List. People on whose radar screen you wish to remain, but who you don't want to take time to meet with again, at least not at this time.

Separate your A List into those contacts whom you can help. Focus first on those you can help in order to form the habit of making giving your first priority. By giving first, you build good will and give your contacts a strong reason to remember you and want to reciprocate. Call or email your contact within a week of your introduction to offer your help. Strike while the memory of your introduction is still fresh. If you wait over two weeks, you will essentially be making a cold call.

Make your move

Plan your strategy. Decide whom to communicate with first. Do you want to call a first generation contact who can deliver precisely what you need? Or would it be better to proceed incrementally, building step by step until you can reach a target who can provide what you want?

Usually, the best and easiest approach is to be straight forward. Send an email similar to the example below:

Hi Bill-

It was great meeting you at the Chamber mixer. Every time I think about that story you told about Frank, I crack up laughing.

Attached is an article on new monitors that might interest you.

Are you free for lunch this Thursday, March 21st. Hope you can make it because it would be fun.

My best to Phil.

Rick

In your follow up communiqué, state where you met and include a reference that will make the connection closer and more personal. Attach or send articles of information, cartoons or information that might interest your contact and open up subjects for future communications. Make sure that whatever you send or attach is relevant, otherwise you'll be sending irritating spam. In your message, refer to shared experiences or special events that occurred.

State your request directly and specifically. If you merely say, "Lets get together for lunch," without suggesting a particular date, it may never happen. By being specific, you shift the responsibility to your contact to either accept or decline and you keep the flow of communications alive.

If you are looking for information, be clear about what you want. State, "When we met at the NSA conference, you mentioned that you have a friend who works for Steve Spielberg and that he might be interested in my screenplay. Can I email him and use your name? If so, please send me his email address."

The immediacy of email makes it ideal for following up. Instead of being forced to wait for the delivery of a letter or note, email is instantaneous ... it's the emailers who take longer. Through email you can quickly set up follow-up appointments or meetings. Notes or letters may be more personal and more appropriated for specific contacts, but email quickly gets the job done and in most cases is perfectly acceptable.

Follow–up phone calls are as fast as email, but busy people are harder to reach by phone. Unlike telephone messages, most emails are usually read and responded to promptly.

To make your follow ups more memorable, attach articles, announcements, cartoons or other information that might interest your contact. Send information related to or of interest to his/her business or concerns. Send joke or gag gifts to get their attention, but don't be a pest. Don't relentlessly inundate your contact with unrequested information or your subsequent communications won't even be opened.

After you send articles or announcements, telephone your contacts. Ask what they think about the item you sent, how could it impact them and ask them to explain it to you from their perspective. Show interest and concern, but don't try to sell them. Simply try to create a positive impression and build for the future. If you can't get through by phone, do it via email.

Professional speaker and marketing consultant Ken Glickman recommends a method of following up that will to create a great impression. When you come across an item that could help a contact, don't immediately fax or email it. Instead, first send an email saying, "I found something very useful and I'm going to send it to you Wednesday." When it arrives on Wednesday, you've accomplished two objectives: (1) you helped your contact by sending something he/she might find valuable and (2) you've demonstrated that you are a person who does as he/she promised. By following Glickman's approach, you can subtly position yourself to create an excellent impression

When you hear about developments related to your contacts, call and ask how it will impact them. Show interest and concern. Again, don't try to sell; simply try to be a friend. When appropriate, ask how you can help.

Always say "thanks"

Whenever some one introduces you, recommends you, endorses you, speaks well of you or helps you in any way, quickly and clearly express your gratitude. Say thanks as soon as possible while you are still enthusiastic and can fully communicated the depths of your feelings.

Thank everyone who has been kind, warm and pleasant or done a good job. Express your appreciation on the spot clearly and let them know how much their assistance means to you.

People remember your thanks; it makes them feel happy that they helped you. When you boil it down, thanking others is recognizing and acknowledging their efforts and, unfortunately, it isn't expressed often enough. Saying thanks costs absolutely nothing and it takes but seconds to state, but provides a great way to make people happy. And, as a result, they will usually remember and think fondly of you. When you make those who help you feel pleased, they will usually make even greater efforts to assist you again.

Expressing your appreciation is an important part of following up. It opens the door for closer, warmer and frequently more productive interactions.

NETWORKING NUGGET

In August 2002, marketing strategist Robyn Levin attended a networking event in Dallas with 500 other women business owners/ entrepreneurs. The event was hosted by eWomenNetwork. Robyn was so impressed with the event that when it was over, she made a point of personally thanking and congratulating Sandra and Kym Yancy, the founders of eWomenNetwork.

Two months later, Robyn was scheduled to attend a wedding in Dallas. So she called Kym to see if they could meet. As a marketing strategist, Robyn is always looking for opportunities to develop strategic alliances to promote products and services for clients and herself. At their meeting, Robyn updated Kym on her ideas to create opportunities for eWomen members and they explored joint marketing ideas including her eBook, *Capsules: Top 25 Tips & Creative Remedies for Women and Small Business Owners*. Over the next few months, Robyn and Kym kept in touch and before long, he invited her to be the eWomenNetwork's West Coast Corporate Alliance Representative, which Robyn happily accepted.

The best, most personal way to show your appreciation is by writing a handwritten note. It doesn't have to be elaborate or on fancy or expensive stationary. Simply expressing your gratitude on a nice note or post card will do fine. People remember, are impressed and touched when you take time from your busy life to thank them. Have you ever received a hand written thank-you note from a powerful person? It makes you feel wonderful, exhilarated and ten-feet tall. It's a wonderful touch that you never forget!

Phone calls can also be effective and personal. They allow you to articulate the full extent of your gratitude and can extend into warm, pleasant and fun filled exchanges. However, phone calls can run on and it can be hard to cut them off without sounding curt.

Email is less personal than notes and phone calls, but is quick. If well written, email can be just as expressive as notes and phone calls. Often, it's better to send a quick, thank-you email than to wait and send the perfect handwritten note. Remember, the method you choose for saying thanks is secondary as long as you say it promptly.

Remember, email can read more harshly than intended. So take great pains to word your emails in softer language. To avoid harshness, some folks send their email to themselves first. They read them and, if they set the proper tone, they forward them to the intended recipient ... but only after they read them first.

To express your thanks for special favors, think about sending a gift. Even old standards like flowers, candy or wine are greatly appreciated, especially when they were not expected. A small gift is a wonderful way to say thanks and be fondly remembered.

In thanking others, as in giving, be generous. Develop the reputation for giving more than is necessary especially of your time and efforts.

Negative responses

If your contact isn't responsive, try to preserve the connection. Things always change and today's rejections could be tomorrow's acceptances so don't abandon the contact. Be patient, but be persistent. Gently remind your contact about yourself without being a pain.

- Send articles or information that might interest your contact and include brief notes that say, "I thought this might interest you. Hope all is well. My best. Phil." Don't overdo it or you will be considered a pest and your communiqués will be avoided. Send only truly relevant information and set the standards for what you send extremely highly.
- If you get an outright rejection, ask, "Who else can you recommend that I can call?" If you receive a name or names, obtain permission to use your contact's name. If he/she agrees, call and say, "Don Martin of the Times suggested that I call you."
- Keep your contacts in the loop. Report on how your dealings with his/her referrals went and clearly express your thanks. Report back whenever you reach a major plateau.
- If you finalize a deal through your contact's referral, send a gift to show your appreciation. You don't have to break the bank or buy a lavish gift, but send something, even a plant, flowers or candy.

Following up is not simply a short-term strategy, it's a critical discipline that is essential in networking. Following up is how you convert leads into lasting network relationships. It's a time-tested method that is critical in building and maintaining productive networks. Following up broadens your contact base; sharpens your skills and impresses others by demonstrating your professionalism, reliability and dedication.

In following up, a delicate balance must be maintained between persistence and pushiness. Although you frequently have to be persistent, be persistent with a light and gentle touch. When you email or call contacts, be warm, friends, fun and grateful. Don't by pushy, overly forceful or aggressive. Approach contacts with soft, little nudges, not atomic warheads. Be patient because if you're too push, you may give you the book to get you off their backs, which is the last thing that you want.

How to follow up

Schedule a regular time each day to follow up, say each morning when you start working. Make following up a part of your daily routine, schedule it like an appointment and enter it on your calendar. Allot a set amount of time to enter contact information and call or email contacts.

In email, summarize the reason you are communicating in the subject line. For example, "Lunch on June 6th." Then elaborate on it more fully in the body of the email message. By identifying the topic in the subject line, your contacts can know the purpose of your communiqué without having to open it and can deal with it at a convenient time.

Keep emails short, don't get wordy. Say just enough to make your clearly make your point.

If you leave a telephone message, state your name first and then say why you are calling. It will provide context for who you are and the reason you are calling. If you call and reach your contact, state your name, ask how he/she is and than say why you called.

- Send email with a return receipt in order to verify that it was received. Also program your email to automatically provide your contact information in a signature file. Signature files appear at the bottom of outgoing emails and list your contact information. In addition to your name, business, address, telephone number, fax number and Web address, signature files can also give your business motto or your sound bite. When sending faxes, include a fax cover sheet that provides the same or similar information that is in your signature file.

- When a contact shows interest and promises to call you back, try to pin him/her down regarding when you can expect the call. If he/she doesn't call within the appointed time, which is likely, call or email to provide him/her with a gentle reminder.

- There will be times when you are not be the right fit for certain contacts. On those occasions, try to salvage something positive by being pleasant and keeping open the channels of communication. If you can't build a business relationship, try to build a friendly relationship. Thank contacts for their time and request the names of others who might help as well as you contacts' permission to say they referred you.

> Steve Lillo, CEO of web design company PlanetLink.com shares a tip for making the follow up process quicker and easier. When he is at an event, he sends an email to the person he's met right after the conversation is still fresh and references some of the specifics of the discussion – often within minutes. He codes the subject of the message for the event so that he can go back through his sent emails and have a record of the people he's contacted. Steve shares that this does two important things for him. It eliminates the need to enter all the contacts at the same time after the event is over and it enhances a positive impression with a quick follow up while still at the event.

Follow up log

Record your follow-up efforts in a log that you can quickly access. Record in the log the date and time of each follow-up attempt, who you contacted, the type of contact (E=email, T=telephone, L=letter, FTF=face to face meeting, etc.), the subject of the contact and the outcome or result. The outcome could be "reached answering machine" or "spoke with Debbie Levick and scheduled lunch for April 5th."

Sample Follow-Up Log

DATE/TIME	*CONTACT*	*SUBJECT*	*TYPE*	*OUTCOME*
2/11/04–9 AM	*Ed Galvez* *Producer*	*Marfa Trip*	*E*	*N/R. Follow up next week*
2/11/04–9:30 AM	*Kate Slavin* *Harpers Bazaar*	*New ads*	*T*	*Spoke, showed interest.*
2/12/04–1 PM	*Jeff Long* *Studio*	*Marfa trip*	*E*	*N/R Follow up on 2/19*
2/14/04–1:30 PM	Weinberg Bros.	Lakers tickets	T	Spoke. Will send
2/14/04–2 PM	Leslie Fleming	Wedding	E	Will meet on 2/17

Many contact managers and CRM systems provide a way for you to take notes and create a record of your contacts as well as to let you schedule a date for future follow up or a date and time for a phone call or meeting.

It gets easier

Believe it or not, with practice, following up gets easier; it even gets to be routine and second nature. As you become more proficient, you'll find that important contacts respect professionalism and prefer to deal with professionals because they know that they can usually rely upon professionals. So when you follow up in a well-planned, disciplined and timely fashion, important contacts might be more willing to deal with you.

Benefits from following up also spill over to other facets of your life. They teach you patience, understanding and diplomacy. They give you a better idea how to plan, position yourself, wait your turn and seize opportunities. Following up isn't just persistence, although you must be persistent, it's being considerate, respectful and wise. It's treating people as you wish to be treated … just like networking.

> On occasions, you'll get lucky. Everybody will ask you to lunch, invite you to their club and introduce you to their A List members. On these lucky streaks, nothing will go wrong and you will be the toast of the town, the "flavor of the month," the person most in demand, with whom everyone wants to be associated. Treat those times with reverence, appreciate your good fortune and realize that they're probably just a temporary phenomena … special, fleeting moments.
>
> When you're on top, leverage your success by treating everyone well. Share your success by being magnanimous. Be kind, understanding, gracious and generous. Help whoever needs help … whether or not they ask, look for opportunities to help. Apply your good fortune, your moment in the sun, to give generously to others.

Rule of seven

In public relations, there is a rule called "the Rule of Seven," which also applies to following up. According to the rule, it takes seven steps, calls or emails, to actually get a booking. "Expect six no's before you get a yes … or, after seven attempts, you many never get a yes and have to move on. Whenever they say no, be gracious. A no may be no for now, but not forever. Never burn bridges." Rick advises.

When you're following up, it may not take seven calls or emails to connect with your contact; he/she may cut you off after just one. Nevertheless, be prepared to make seven honest attempts. If, after giving it seven whole-hearted tries, you haven't connected, move on. Rethink your options and go to Plan B. Move that contact to your C List. Drop him/her an occasional email or postal mailing to remain on his/her radar screen, but bypass him/her and get on with your life.

Although your contact may not need or want to see you now, be professional. Proceed with dignity and respect for your contact's time. Networking is a long-term process, not just quick hit or miss shot. It's about how you live your life, how you treat others and most people will notice. By being understanding, patient and principled, doors will remain open for you and sometime in the future you could connect.

When you receive rejections, when contacts don't respond favorably, don't become discouraged or upset. Don't get angry or give up. Instead, turn to other sources, focus your energy on other contacts and keep on plugging! Building and maintaining relationships takes patience, persistence and principles. It also takes following up, following up, following up … but it can get you the pot of gold.

Advocates' list

List the top 25 individuals who provide you with business and are members of your inner circle. Business advisor Mark LeBlanc calls this your advocate's list because the people on this list will really go to bat for you. The people on your advocates' list are your prime supporters. They won't just call their contacts to recommend you, they will call and set up meetings or try to convince their contacts that they can't live or stay in business without hiring you or using your product or services.

Every month, send the 25 members on your advocates' list something that will remind them about you, LeBlanc advises. It doesn't have to be elaborate or expensive, just enough to make the recipients think positively of you. For example you can send a simple email greeting, a newsletter, an article, a cartoon, statistical information, a copy of your book or a discount for using your product or service. Constantly look for interesting and fun items that you can send your advocates.

At least once each year, contact everyone listed in your database. Send letters for special occasions such as Christmas, the New Year, birthdays, anniversaries, Thanksgiving, tax time, your favorite hero's birthday or invent some other reason. Let them know that you're still around, still in business and that you're thinking of them.

When you contact the members of your advocates' list or database via postal mail, score extra points by personalizing your communications with the addition of a short, handwritten note or comment. Taking the time and making the effort to add, "Hope all is well!," "Miss seeing you!" or "How about lunch soon?," will go a long way to rekindling and maintaining important relationships.

★ ★ ★ Action steps ★ ★ ★

1. Identify four contact management systems or software programs or CRM systems to investigate for your use.

_____

_____

_____

_____

2. Set forth the criteria for contacts to be included on your A List.

_____

_____

_____

_____

3. Compose a standard thank you note that you could adapt to send or email your appreciation.

_____

_____

_____

_____

4. *List three ways that you can follow up with contacts who do not respond to your approaches.*

_____

_____

_____

CHAPTER 11

MINING THE INTERNET

"National borders aren't even speed bumps
on the information superhighway."
—Tim May, Ontologist

- ❑ *Web sites*
- ❑ *Clipping services*
- ❑ *Media calendar services*
- ❑ *Internet communities*
- ❑ *Blogs*
- ❑ *Signature files*
- ❑ *Social media*
- ❑ *Mailing lists (move mailing lists under websites at the top of the list)*
- ❑ *The KickSugar group*

According to estimates, nearly 3 billion people worldwide use or have access to the Internet. As a result, the Internet has become a networker's paradise because it enables networkers to link up with a virtually unlimited array of potential networking partners across the globe.

David Hancock told us, "I live in the present. I am well aware of the past, very enticed by the future, but the here and now is where I reside, embracing the technologies of the present and leaving future technologies on the horizon right where they belong. I am alert to the new, wary of the avant-garde, and wooed from the old only by improvement, not mere change. Having said that, I do utilize social networking, but am very aware of the precious nature of time so I don't spend unproductive time on those networks. I also utilize tools like TimeTrader.com and Timebridge.com to help manage my calendar and set up easy conference calls with prospects and clients. I make sure to keep my profiles current and relevant in business sites like LinkedIn, Plaxo and others."

In the past, when you wanted to network, you were restricted to regional or industry-specific efforts. Usually, you had to network in your own community and try to build from there. A certain, select few were able to attend state or national trade shows, conferences or conventions and could network within their own industry. However, most of these events were costly and they took place only a few times each year. Building close relationships with contacts in other states or countries was difficult and expensive so most networkers stayed close to home.

Now, it is all changed because the Internet recognizes few boundaries. In fact, the Internet erases most boundaries.

- Web site and Internet communities now blanket the world. When you visit a site or take part in an Internet community, you don't know whether it emanates from across the hall or across the ocean. You may end up chatting with people who live abroad or down the street. You can communicate with, learn from and do business with individuals who have vast experience in a field you may have just entered.

- The Internet's global reach dramatically increases your networking possibilities. By simply joining an Internet community, you can be surrounded by scores of like-minded people who are eager to discuss subjects that interest you and share their information, resources and insights.

- As a networking tool, the Internet is an exceptional value because you don't have to pay steep admission fees or the expenses that mount up when you attend networking groups and events. When you network via the Internet, you don't have to shave, comb your hair or even get out of your PJs. You can sit at home, safe and snug and network with multiple, faceless partners in cyberspace.

Web sites

It is vital to build a dynamic, information-based web site. Fill it with the precise information that you would like the world to know about you, your product or service. Use your Web site to paint a striking picture that will intrigue potential network partners and attract them to you.

> In constructing your website, be careful because a bad site is often worse than having no website. So make your website good. Make it better than good, make it great, because a great website will make you look good and give your visitors a positive impression of who you are and what you do. A site that lacks quality content, that is poorly designed or difficult to navigate, will alienate visitors. Not only won't they revisit your site, they will complaint about it to others.

In designing your Web site, decide:

- Who constitutes your target audience
- What is the best way to reach them
- What information they will need

Don't put your Web site up until it's well tested and you are absolutely sure that it is:

(1) Easy to use
(2) Informative, clearly stating the benefits of your business offerings

(3) Attractive

(4) Reflective of your mission

(5) Quick to download

1. **Easy to use**. Visitors are busy and they're not patient. If your site isn't easy to navigate, they won't spend time trying to figure it out. Instead, they'll abandon you and go somewhere else. Visitors can also be fickle so make your site easy and intuitive to use. If using your site isn't totally painless for visitors to use, they will flee in droves and probably never come back.

Before launching your site:

- Test it on friends or family members who are short on computer/Web experience
- Note the problems they encounter
- Assume that others will incur the same problems and that the problems are with your site, not with your visitors
- Don't accept excuses or explanations from Web designers. Care only that your site is easily navigable by anyone from novices to experts. Be firm, the bottom line is that the site should be easy to use
- Make sure that your site works smoothly with all operating systems and browsers
- Properly fix all problems

When your site is up, continually monitor it to be sure that all problems have been cured and that all links work smoothly. If your site doesn't work, visitors won't return … count on it.

2. **Informative**. Your Web site must be informative and contain the information that visitors want. Design attracts visitors and ease of operation keeps them happy, but valuable content brings them back. Find out beforehand exactly what your target audience wants and build your site to give it to them. Include an area of your site that

has continually updated content—an integrated blog is a great way to easily provide updated content.

Show visitors who you are, what information you provide and how it can benefit them. Give them strong reasons to deal with you. Describe your business, your business history, your financial data and what you accomplished for your customers/clients. Be completely honest and never exaggerate. Think about the ruined careers that were caused by inflated resumes. Include customer/client testimonials and endorsements.

On your site, display your portfolio, staff biographies, staff photographs, customer/client lists, news, newsletters, games, promotions, special offers, contests, privacy and security policies and links to other sites. Include product descriptions, product specifications, price lists, photographs, illustrations, audio, video, ordering information, shipping instructions, direct e-mail links or a form for questions, comments or for ordering goods or services.

3. **Attractive**. A Web site is an electronic show room that the world at large can enter, inspect and critique. It's also an extension of you and the manner that you choose to project yourself.

Your site should be so attractive to your target audience that it grabs your visitors' attention and makes them to respond positively to you, your product or service. It should make them look forward to returning to your site and recommending it to others.

Design—a site's look and feel ... is the first thing that visitors notice. It's like your sound bite, your first impression and it's often what visitors remember most. Visitors react to a site's look and feel before they explore its content. If the site is attractive, easy to read and use, visitors may continue to explore, but if it's not, they'll head for the hills.

Site design reflects how you want to be perceived. It can be classical, traditional, modern, progressive, avant-garde, etc. Bold design featuring unusual colors, color combinations and typefaces can signify a dynamic, aggressive and vigorous approach. However, it can also be disconcerting, visual noise that will turn visitors off before they examine your content. Its vital that your website accurately represent your brand. The design of your Web site will influence how visitors react to you, your product or service.

From time to time, vary your site's look. Add and subtract, make changes. Try to keep your site fresh and exciting. Think of it as a gallery that continually mounts new shows rather than a museum that always displays its permanent collection.

Web design isn't just about looks. It also controls other essential features including the site's structure, organization and ease of navigation.

4. **Reflective of your mission**. The main reason why your Web site exists is to support your mission. It should support and reflect the mission of your business or whatever you're trying to promote. If the mission of your business is to sell candy, create a mouth-watering site that makes visitors salivate and feel like biting into images on the screen. Clearly describe your candy and make it a snap for visitors to buy online.

5. **Quick to download.** Even if visitors are just browsing, they hate to waste their time. "The site took too long to download," is a consistent complaint that Web designer Steve Lillo of PlanetLink (www. planetlink.com) hears. According to Steve, slowness is a major turn off. A slow website is also a detriment to your search engine rankings. Successful Web sites download fast. If visitors have to wait, most will go to other sites if they have the option, they might even turn to your competitors. Today, Web sites can be built to download fast and look great so don't accept lame excuses. Make sure that your site functions well on mobile devices—more and more visitors are accessing your website with a mobile device.

Web designers know how to best use color, optimize and compress images and judiciously incorporate graphics to make your site "lean and mean" and still visually shine. They can write code that tells your browser how the web page looks while taking minimal space and sparingly using downloadable files. Web designers also understand that if you have regular corporate customers, you many not need slow-loading pictures or graphics.

Web designer, Steve Lillo (www.planetlink.com) shared his secrets on how to assure that visitors to your site come back. They are:

- Always tell the truth. State the facts clearly and avoid hype, buzz words and jargon. If you're stating your opinion, make it crystal clear that you're merely giving your opinion, not quoting facts.

- Employ appropriate technology to insure that every element of your site is easy to use. Keep in mind that use of the latest technology doesn't always produce the most effective Web site. Ease of use is especially important with large, complex sites. Make sure all links connect properly.

- Make your site lively and entertaining. Create great content that visitors will look forward to reading. Give advice, the latest news and explain "how-to." Include anecdotes, jokes, industry gossip, tips, contests, surveys and discussion groups. Award prizes and give discounts on merchandise.

- Keep content updated so that the information you provide is always correct. Remember your Web site is a research tool. Visitors will depend on you for reliable information and won't use your site if your information isn't current. Provide information that's updated regularly such as daily tips or monthly articles.

- Notify people via e-mail about significant news developments, updates to your site and other information that may be of benefit or interest to them. Create a link from the e-mail to your site so those interested can easily access your site. Provide a way for your visitors to sign up on your mailing list and give them an incentive for doing so—a report, ebook, video or other downloadable file. Stay in touch with them and make sure to provide take-away value in your email so that they'll want to open your messages.

- Deliver what you promise … if you can't deliver it, don't promise. As previously stressed, results are ultimately what count and once you get past the glitter, results are what visitors to your site want. If you don't provide as advertised, you'll lose credibility and most likely your business.
- Update the look of your Web site so it's consistent with your other marketing materials. Periodically freshen it by changing colors, type, graphics and layouts.
- Never litter the Web with spam. Don't host or use services that specialize in circulating spam. The wide distribution they offer is more than offset by the resentment they arouse. Sending spam can also cause you to lose your account, which can result in lost business.
- Provide added value. Find out what information or services you provide that will cause visitors to return to your site and include it. Fill your site with newsletters, industry analysis, calendars of events, industry directories and other interactive services. Create a Web site that visitors will want to return to and recommend.

Mailing lists

An email mailing list provides a way to stay in touch with visitors to your website as well as existing and previous customers, and individuals that you've met in your other networking activities. As we mentioned above, provide a form on your website for visitors to provide their name and email address in exchange for receiving a bonus. The CANSPAM Act, which was passed by the United States Congress in response to the overwhelming amount of junk email specifically states that to be in compliance, anyone on your email list needs to be someone whom you have an existing relations ship or has opted into your list.

On your website, have a form for visitors to fill out in order to receive something for free—an ebook, report, white paper, audio or video are all good choices. Their name and email address is stored in a database system for sending emails. In Chapters 6 and 10, we mentioned CRM systems for keeping track of our contacts. Many CRM systems also provide mailing list services. There are also services that provide the mailing list functionality without the CRM, generally for a lower cost. For small number you could send emails from your email account. This isn't a good solution for more than a handful of email addresses thought because of group emails being limited and blocked because of spam safeguards.

Online clipping services

Clipping services keep track of the media's coverage of specific industries and areas of interests. They save you the time and energy of scouring media to find articles and information of interest to you, your network targets and partners. They give you the ability to check out a wider range of media sources than you could review on your own.

By using clipping services to monitor what is going on in your industry, you can gather information to distribute to your network partners so that they can understand what you do and find opportunities for you. Clipping services are also ideal for collecting information of about your network targets' and your network partners' interests so that you can identify leads and be more valuable to them.

A number of clipping services exist. They include:

- Bacon's Information, Inc.-—www.cision.com
- CyberAlert—www.cyberalert.com
- eWatch—www.ewatch.com
- BurrellesLuce—www.burrelleslluce.com
- Webclipping.com—www.webclipping.com
- Google Alerts—www.google.com/alerts

Media calendar services

Another valuable online tool is media calendar services. These services provide searchable databases of items on editorial calendars and contact information for editorial personnel from thousands of publications.

So if you are looking for information to supply to a target or to one of your network partners, you can check whether items in their fields of interest are listed on upcoming editorial calendars. Calendar services provide editorial profiles for publications including their editorial thrust and target audience. They also give you access to contact information for the editorial personnel involved in forthcoming pieces. Media calendar databases are searchable by topic, keyword, publication name, circulation and location.

Online calendar services include:

- Lexis/Nexis Press Files—lexisnexis.com/pressaccess/pressfiles
- Media Map—www.EdCals.com

Online Communities

According to estimates, hundred of thousands of online communities now exist ... discussion groups, newsgroups, mailing lists, bulletin boards, message boards, chat rooms, etc. Internet communities are interactive forums where members with similar interests exchange ideas and information. Although the term "discussion group" usually denotes a two-way conversation and the other terms refer to one-way dialogs, in this book, we'll simply use the term "discussion groups" to refer to all online communities and groups.

Discussion groups are ideal for networking because they basically are networks. They are electronic groups that share information and opinions on areas of mutual interest. Discussion group members can come from all over the world to conduct electronic conversations, build relationships and help one another. In discussion groups, members network by:

- Exploring solutions to problems of mutual interest
- Demonstrating their expertise
- Building relationships
- Building reputations
- Learning and
- Helping one another

Online discussion groups can expand your existing networks and link you with network partners throughout the world. Group members can post and respond to comments or simply sit back and silently observe. When you join a discussion group, you generally don't know the other members: who they are, what they do and why they're in the group. But as you get more deeply involved, group members become friends, confidants, mentors, advisors and valuable network partners.

Before joining an online community, answer the same questions that you asked when designing your Web site:

1.   Who constitutes your target audience?
2.   What is the best way to reach them?
3.   What information they will need? and

Decide whom you want to connect with who could help you the most. What industries they are in? Are there certain discussion groups within those industries that you could join? Identify the areas of your network that are weak and then identify groups in those areas that you could join to get you up to speed. To find discussion groups, see:

- www.groups.google.com
- www.groups.yahoo.com
- www.topica.com

Online discussion groups can provide you with substantial information that can be invaluable to you and your network partners. You can lurk, or silently monitor discussion groups, to learn what customers and clients are saying about your or your network partners' product or service and similar products and services. Monitoring discussion groups will also give you a feel for:

- Marketplace trends and conditions
- Needs and concerns of your network partners
- Problems with products and services

- How problems can be corrected
- Ideas for new products and applications and rumors or
- Misinformation that you can dispel

Submit your own questions to discussion groups to get valuable feedback and to find kindred spirits. Through feedback you can identify potential network partners.

Posting

Before posting items or even participate in a discussion group, follow the group for several days, at the least. Learn their rules, conventions, whether the group includes your target audience and if so, their needs. Each group is different and groups constantly evolve as the take and lose members and as changes in their areas of interest occur.

Know your group! When you post an item to a discussion group, you're essentially placing yourself in a conversation, you're entering a community where the residents have established their own structures and rules.

- Be sure that you like the group. Does it include members who you would value as network partners? Do the members share your interests? Are they too gossipy, too technical or not serious enough about business? Are they too expert, advanced, cynical, critical, naive or unsophisticated? Do you feel comfortable in the group? If not, try another group . . . there are plenty out there!
- Before blindly jumping in a discussion group and posting the first thing that enters your mind, get a feel for how the group members conduct themselves. Familiarize yourself with the type and style of their postings and learn the group's rules. If your postings violate the group's rules, you could lose your posting rights or irritate members. Irate members have been known to retaliate by bombarding violators with hostile messages called flames.
- Find out the group's policies on advertising and promotion and don't violate them. Many groups do not accept advertising or blatant self-

promotion. However, the screening tends to be loose or nonexistent prohibited ads are run.

- If you try to slip in a prohibited ad, hordes of angry, even vicious, e-mailers could attack you. The can make your life miserable and boycott you, your product, service or Web site. They could even launch hate campaigns against you. So follow the rules and be careful not to alienate group members.

Most discussion groups are intended to inform, not to sell or promote and in extending your network, that's what you want. Again, the ticket is giving generously without expectation of return. Monitor postings to learn what they need and then try to fulfill those needs. Concentrate on building relationships and don't try to sell. To avoid boycotts or hate campaigns:

- Edit and rewrite pieces to comply with the group's rules
- Minimize the commercial aspects and to maximize the informational aspects
- Comment, answer questions and make recommendations to build relationships, expand your network and enhance your credibility
- Demonstrate your knowledge, expertise and willingness to help
- Provide help generously

Before you try to connect group members with your other contacts, get the group members' okay and explain the reasons why you think the connection would be beneficial.

If you make a close contact in the group, you have the option of communicating with that person in a private message. Private messages go the individual's email address not to the group.

Signature files

Unless the rules of the group prohibit it, add a signature file at the end of all postings to discussion groups as well as to all for your outgoing emails. A signature file contains your name, the name of your business and your contact information. It can also include your sound bite or business message as in Jill's signature file below.

Jill Lublin, CEO

Influence Marketing

Author, National Best-Seller Guerrilla Publicity

Syndicated Radio Host, Do The Dream

(415) 883-5455

http://www.Jilllublin.com

"It's not who you know, it's who knows you!"

Link your signature file to your Web site. It can build your traffic by providing a way for visitors to get to your site as well as by increasing your search engine ranking.

Read the signature files of the members who post items in your discussion groups. When responding to their postings, ask about their business, interests, sound bites or slogans. Check their Web sites to learn more about them.

Blogging

In addition to having your own blog, there are two additional ways that you can leverage the power of blogging—guest posts and commenting.

Guesting posting is essentially writing a post that someone will include in his or her blog. A guest post is an opportunity to share your expertise with a new audience. It's a great way to get extra exposure that you wouldn't have otherwise. The greater that value you can provide, the more likely your guest post will be accepted for publication. Search for blogs that have a target audience that is an overlap for your target audience where your skills talent and expertise can be of benefit. Include a brief bio, your byline, at the end of your post that includes some information about your qualifications. Often the post can include a link back to your website in your author byline. Contact the author and ask if there would be interested in you providing a guest post for their blog. Provide your post to them with no expectation of receiving something in return from them. You're providing them content and they're providing you exposure.

Many blogs also allow comments. Be very careful to provide a real response in your comment. Don't just make a comment so that you can include a link to your website—that doesn't present you as an expert or authority and is likely to get you banned from commenting on other blogs. Think about what you can add to the conversation—an experience, perspective or point of view that adds to the discussion is always valuable.

Social media

LinkedIn, Facebook, Twitter and Google+, are only some of websites for social media that are available to the savvy networker. The number of tools available to automate, optimize and interconnect your social media footprint can be mind-boggling. Resist the urge to try to do the all at the same time. Start with one and learn how to use it effectively. Add another site later after you've become comfortable with it and you're posting regularly. Social media can be great for making new connections, building credibility and cross-pollinating with new groups.

Social media is a great way to establish and present yourself as an expert and authority in your field. By providing your expertise without being self-promotional, you drawn attention and recognition to get people to notice who your are. Speak with truth, authority and humility while truly being helpful. Social media is about building and strengthening relationships and is an important tool in your Networking toolbox.

The KickSugar group

When journalist Connie Benesch discovered that her health problems, bouts of moodiness and other erratic behavior were due to severe hypoglycemia and sugar intolerance, she eliminated all sugar from her diet. A few years later, she decided to write *SUGAR SHOCK!* Like millions of other Internet users, Benesch also began exploring the world of networking online by joining several discussion groups. On the Internet, Benesch found a way to instantly connect with other hypoglycemics and sugar addicts grappling with similar problems.

Realizing the tremendous potential of networking online, Benesch founded and began moderating her own discussion group, the KickSugar group (Subscribe: kicksugar-subscribe@yahoogroups.com). Her goals for both the group and her book were the same—to inspire, educate and help those who were also suffering from sugar intolerance. Benesch wanted to support sufferers who were enduring the same mysterious symptoms that had tormented her for years and to let them know that they were not alone. The group, in turn, gave Benesch direct access to her target audience, fellow sugar intolerants, who by voicing their concerns enabled her to discover the type of information they wanted in a book.

Benesch started the KickSugar group in November 2002 and an average of 20 new members have joined each month (including those who have dropped out). Its members are from all over the US, Canada and several foreign nations. The questions group members ask have identified their major concerns and their comments are filled with revealing insights and valuable information.

"In my mind, this KickSugar group has been a mutually rewarding experience. I like to think that members of my virtual community have been inspired, nurtured and supported in ways that they haven't found in the 'real world.' I could be wrong, but, in my opinion, we can network online in a way that doesn't seem to exist in real time. Members of my group have said as much to me and to the group," Benesch noted.

"In part, the anonymity we have online allows us to share in very deep, meaningful ways. Both shy and gregarious people alike can discuss topics easily—with no fear of people frowning at them or looking at them askance. I suspect that it's easier for most people to reveal their fears, worries and suspicions in a supportive, online home than it would be in a room full of people."

Benesch makes it clear to everyone that she is not a physician, but she did bring in a registered dietician to work closely with her group. Benesch believes that her lay status and personal history of sugar problems are actually a bonus because the group would not be as open and forthcoming if she were a physician or a scientist writing a book about the dangers of sugar.

Like any relationship, the KickSugar group had evolved and its nature has changed. It was originally designed to be small, but now has well over 100 members because Benesch didn't have the heart to turn away suffering people who came to the group for help.

A smaller, private group has spun off from the KickSugar group. It consists of seven members who write to each other and to the group's consulting dietician each day to report what they eat and what affect these foods have on how they feel. The dietician analyzes their intake and she and the subgroup make suggestions and observations. Benesch also belongs to a hypoglycemia group as well as to a private group composed of authors and experts who network and share information.

Why members join

Members join the KickSugar group to receive help, support, encouragement, information and inspiration. They form deep, intricate and supportive relationships with each other and Benesch. Members seem to like the on line camaraderie and enjoy being a part of a sharply focused virtual community.

The biggest benefit, according to Benesch, is that members realize that they are not alone in their struggles, which gives them enormous relief. They also benefit greatly from having a knowledgeable, non-stop, ever-present, support team as close as their keyboard.

In their battle against sugar, group members are at all different stages. They range from struggling beginners who want to learn more about symptoms that plague them, to those who need support in staying off sugar to others who have been off sugar for a while and want to help others. Members also include people diagnosed as hypoglycemic and diabetic as well as obese and overweight individuals. Benesch stresses that the idea that only overweight people have sugar-related problems is totally false.

How to start a Yahoo Group

A number of sites host discussion groups in addition to Yahoo. Meetup, LinkedIn, Ryze, Ning and Google+ all provide tools for groups to interact and exchange information or resources. Starting and joining a Yahoo Group is free. Founders of groups can choose to open them to the public, as Benesch has or keep them private. Public groups are listed at http://dir.groups.yahoo.com/dir. Private groups are for members only and are unlisted. Many people find out about groups by word of mouth.

To start your own Yahoo Group, you need to get a user ID. After signing on, you simply go to http://groups.yahoo.com/start. Yahoo has a few requirements, but none are onerous. Since Benesch was writing a book and wanted people to remember her, she used her own name as her user ID. In addition, to start a group you must create a group description and set the group's parameters.

Rules

KickSugar has few rules.

- Attachments were outlawed after some attachments to postings inadvertently contained viruses. Most discussion groups ban attachments
- Postings must stick to the topic, but Benesch tries to give members a little leeway
- If a member mentions a study or a news article, he/she has to state who conducted the study or the publication in which the article appeared. This last rule helps confine the group to credible studies and keep discussions at a higher level
- Members cannot make medical claims and each posting contains a medical disclaimer

Moderating a group

The moderator has to set the tone for the group. Benesch doesn't try to convince members to kick sugar completely unless they want to. However, she hopes that they will cut down considerably and find what works for them. The purpose of the KickSugar group is to raise awareness about the dangers of sugar and the decision on whether to stop, cut back or continue is up to each member. Benesch tries to be accepting and encouraging of all points of views and all paths to get there. However, she discourages members from whining because she wants them find the group to be an empowering, if not liberating, experience.

Benesch confesses that she had to learn to be an online leader. When conducting an Internet discussion, you don't get immediate feedback and emails can be misconstrued.

To keep the group lively and relevant, Benesch posts tips and topics for discussions, many of which relate to subjects she addresses in her book. People new to the group often post questions that have been well covered, so Benesch has developed and posted articles that answer these questions and she informs new group members about the availability of this material when they join.

The KickSugar group knows that Benesch is writing a book about the dangers of sugar. When members post pithy or eloquent remarks on topics that the author is covering in her book, she will send them a private email to obtain their permission to use the quote and to explain that it could help others.

Yahoo group members can read group email in three ways. In: (1) separate, individual email, (2) one or more daily digests that lump together all email to the group or (3) on the group's Web site.

When you set up a group on Yahoo, you can have email sent automatically. For example, Benesh has created an introductory email that is sent to people who express interest in joining the group. In that email, she asks would-be-members to briefly explain their goals for joining the group. Although it's an extra and time-consuming step, it gives her a sense about the prospective member. Benesch has also created a number of other emails that are sent automatically: one welcomes new members and another is sent to all members every two weeks asking for ideas to improve the group.

Benesch recommends

Making sure that you have profound dedication to group's mission and the members' goals. "Moderating a discussion group is very time consuming. You have to have a passion and total commitment to your topic or subject matter. It must drive you," Benesch points out. She also notes that moderating a discussion group is a responsibility. "People rely upon you and look up to you and you really need to set a good example."

Benesch also suggests finding a partner or co-moderator to help divvy up the work. "It's a huge commitment of time and you might want to have someone administrate the group."

Benesch finds that the online forum encourages members and allows them to show their vulnerabilities. I find the nature of networking and sharing is different in cyberspace. "When we communicate online in my group, we tend to share intimate thoughts and concerns. Even the most shy will reveal his or her concerns. And we know, without a doubt, that no matter what we say, we'll be unconditionally accepted," Benesch said.

For a list of recommended resources for the tools, websites and services mentioned in this chapter, visit networking-magic.com/resources.

Real World Networking In Our Technological World

In ten years the world appears to have dramatically changed and now people can hardly remember how they survived without Smart-Phones, Facebook, LinkedIn etc. Increasingly, those skills that worked ten years ago to create meaningful business relationships are now looked on as "snail Mail" compared to email or text messaging. Yet after years of explosive growth and acceptance of technology in our lives a backlash is starting to raise its head.

Ultimately, Jean Baptiste said it best when he stated, "The more things change the more they remain the same." Our basic human needs have not changed that much in a thousand years, let alone the last ten years. People still search for meaning and love in their lives, but often define them by the number of friends on Facebook or likes accumulated via their posts.

We are greater networked together, around the globe, then ever before in the history of mankind and yet, we have perhaps never been more out of touch with one another. Increasingly we are hiding behind our phones, computers and fancy social networking platforms. From business networking to online dating we are becoming less comfortable with face-to-face inter personal communications and in-person investments of time and emotional bonding.

We have asked of our technology to take away the risks and time investments of being in direct touch with one another, and we are now living in a world where we are separated from real bonding by the same tools that were meant to help us connect.

Jeff Kahn, CSO of AudioCodes says, "After several months of emails and fancy videoconferences I watched the relationship of a significant global technological alliance that I had initiated grind to a near halt. It was then that I decided to fly all the way around the globe to have several very short meetings with senior execs of one of America's larger and well-known high tech companies. My objective was simply to explain to them that their reliance on the use of fancy video conferencing technology and non-face to face communications like emails was not effectively moving the initiatives between our two companies along at all. The investments that I made on a personal and professional level in order to meet face to face with them was worth the agony of sitting on a plane for countless hours and ultimately solve the problem."

Without even realizing it, we have walked through the "looking glass" and we now serve our technologies more then they serve us. We have become slaves to our Smart Phones, Computers, Tablets and Social Networks. One only need look at how the inclusion of Smart Phones in our lives has dramatically influenced interpersonal communications. How many times have we sat in business meetings where everyone was on his or her smart phone and faked listening to the conversation in the room? How many times have we heard from a loved one that we need to put down the phone and look at them when they are speaking with us? It is time to make the shift back to focusing on the person, not the device.

With that in mind, consider these vital tools to balancing your dependence on technology against the need for face-to-face communication:

Rule #1: Be Present

The challenge of the High Tech/High Touch balancing act is best demonstrated in our use of Smart Phones during meetings. Imagine that while you are now able to utilize your Smart Phone to extend your "presence" to another location and be in touch with someone across the street or across the globe. You could be in a Board meeting but still in touch with your daughter who needed advice about school or you could be with your spouse discussing your upcoming vacation and yet still be in touch with the guys at work about the upcoming product launch.

The idea of being able to be in more then one place at one time is very attractive, however the challenge is that while you succeeded in being present somewhere else you are not fully present where you are or with the people around you at that moment. If you now continue on this path, no matter where you are your "presence" will always be pulled in another direction to the detriment of the person with which you are meeting. It is easy to surmise that the first golden rule of successful interpersonal networking would be simply to be "present."

We are simply lying to ourselves if we begin to believe that we can build "real" relationships only based on Technology.

Rule #2: Build Relationships not Transactional Platforms

The new breed of Technocratic business managers and Social Networkers focus on the creation and management of transactions not relationships. Even the concept of the Facebook "like" has a transactional reality, which is disconnected from the dynamics of healthy Human interpersonal interactions. People post that their Grandfather passed away and then they wait to see the "likes" as if they are receiving a numeric reconfirmation of their value to their "friends."

Lets think of networking as building bridges to other people that can offer potentially valuable either professional or personal opportunity. Now consider that not all bridges are equal and some can handle more traffic and weight then others. Similarly not all networking requests or value demands are equal either.

For example, on a professional level a simple request to forward the name of your designer is not a "heavy" value demand. However, a personal reference to a very important and valuable contact of yours very well be considered a "heavy" request as it effects your creditability. When a bridge is built between two contacts that is based on real relationship building the result is more often then not a "bridge" which can support a flow of "heavy" traffic. Transactional bridges focused on only what was needed from one another and not oriented towards building a relationship a very flimsy and narrow bridge builders.

Max Ernst said it best "Technology is the art of arranging life so we don't have to experience it." Networking is now increasingly done thru Facebook and LinkedIn and countless other apps and platforms. A whole generation has now grown up where the basic social interaction skills are foreign to them and they are petrified about the risks of engaging face to face. We know how to be 24/7 available and multi process, which means we can SMS while we are checking our Facebook posts while having conversations with our loved ones and peers.

This is to say that when in Alice in Wonderland they said, "you might as well say that I get what I like is the same as I get what I like." We have now accepted these plastic exchanges as real and the real world as outdated. Today people get thousands of emails they cannot read or respond to. In fact, very few of us will not admit to being much more moved and focused if we were to receive a hand written or typed letter that was mailed to us. Networking is a people skill and as such it is better in person then via LinkedIn or Facebook, no matter how many bells and whistles they might brag about.

The point here is not to diminish the value of technology. The advent of social networking, smartphones, computers, and other portable devices saves time, allows an undeniable level of connectivity and information to be exchanged, and has literally reinvented the way in which we communicate with one another. However, it is important to note that technology should be used an accelerator for a relationships already built on foundationally viable means. There is simply no substitution for spending time together in the same room. In some measures, our society has shifted the equilibrium to one reliant on technology. However, the most successful networkers out there are the ones that can turn off the phone, disconnect, and build a networking relationship by sitting across the table from one another.

★☆★ Action steps ★☆★

1. Identify the three target audiences that you would like your Web site or discussion group to attract.

_____

_____

_____

2. List the information that your target audiences would need.

_____

_____

_____

3. Set forth the best ways to reach your target audiences.

_____

_____

_____

4. State what you, as a discussion group member, would you want the group to provide for you.

_____

_____

_____

CHAPTER 12

SURVEY SAYS—
NETWORKING DOS

"When a man tells you that he got rich
through hard work, ask him: 'Whose?'"
—**Don Marquis**, Humorist

In our research for this book, we surveyed a wide range of experienced networkers to uncover what they considered the most essential requirements for successful networking. The top, most frequently expressed responses are listed below. Please note that the list below does not place the responses that we received in the order that the respondents indicated were the most important. Instead, they have been arranged to provide a logical, orderly sequence that tracks the networking process.

1. Believe that networking will work. Unless you are truly convinced you're your networking efforts will help you succeed, you will waste everyone's time. Networking requires a positive attitude. A positive attitude will energize you and those around you. Positive energy translates into enthusiasm, which is contagious. When you believe in what you are doing, others will be inspired. Your belief in your cause will convince them to help you and to spread your message to others.

People sense when you are not a true believer; they know when they are being jobbed. Savvy networkers will avoid you because they prefer to deal with those who share their faith in networking rather than wasting their time with those who are insincere and do not. People are usually eager to help; they receive satisfaction from helping others **succeed and if they believe you, they will help.**

2. Target the right audience. Approach individuals who can provide what you seek or who can direct you to those who can. Spend time carefully selecting and researching your targets. Then make a plan to meet them.

If you plan to join groups and/or attend events, select those that target the people you want to reach. Get involved with several different network groups because a single group may not be able to satisfy all your needs, but don't spread yourself too thin. Sample different organizations and events in order to meet a different cross section of people, but give them a chance. Circulating your name widely, putting it in play in a number of arenas, can be extremely helpful.

3. Make a strong first impression. Always put your best foot forward. Be well groomed, dress appropriately and be well prepared. You don't get a second chance to make a first impression and a bad first impression can be ruinous.

Dress appropriately for those you hope to impress. Have a great sound bite, know your stuff and be prepared to reel it off at any time and with confidence. Have a longer description about you or your business down pat that you can quickly recite in the event you are asked about it.

4. Network with those you emulate. Don't be afraid to approach people who you admire and who inspire you. Soot for the top. Meeting those who have achieved your goals gives you a blueprint to learn from and follow. Aim high and seek out those who will help you develop and grow. People at the top can be generous with their help and usually are flattered that you admire and seek their assistance.

While shooting for the top, don't abandon your peers. Your peers can teach you and be supportive. They can act as sounding boards and champion your causes. So continue and nurture peer friendships.

5. Talk to everyone you meet. Don't discount or overlook any one. Be genuinely friendly. People remember your kindnesses to them and will go out of their way reciprocate. When you give of yourself, even it it's only by talking to someone briefly, you re enhancing the possibility of building a relationship and getting something back.

Develop a wide circle of friends and acquaintances from diverse fields. They will fill in your gaps and bring you to new and exciting areas that can broaden your life.

6. Learn to read people. Pay close attention and become skilled at sensing people's needs. Learn to recognize who will give and who will only take. Trust your instincts and when they prove correct, increase your reliance on them. Learn to avoid those who only want to take because they will drain your time and energy. Plus, they are not individuals with whom you want to associate or be affiliated.

7. Listen. Pay carefully attention to what others say. Listen and observe more than talk. Listening can be an acquired skill, so work on becoming a good listener.

Be a good audience and learn about those with whom you speak. Come away knowing one thing they like and one thing they dislike. If you keep them chatting about themselves, they will think you are one of the most interesting people they have met. Ask about their accomplishments before you tell them about yours. Be interested and curious. Don't take yourself too seriously, but take others very seriously.

8. Be willing to help. Give, give, give. Networking is a two way street. Offer your help freely and generously. Think first about how you can help others. When others realize that you are willing to help them and how generous you are, they will be eager to help you. Always keep your contacts' needs in mind and be alert for leads for your network partners. Go the extra mile to provide something special before asking for anything in return. Remember, networking is not only about you.

"The core of networking is finding out how you can help others achieve their goals," according to Dave Sherman, who bills himself as "The Networking Guy." "The reason most people are not successful networkers is that they prospect, instead of networking. Prospecting is the process of finding people to sell your product or service to. Networking is being a valuable business and personal resource for others and EXPECTING NOTHING IN RETURN. The people that give the most will ALWAYS receive the most."

9. Be prepared. Become an expert, be able to provide insightful answers to questions on your field. Know about the places and situations in which you place yourself. Prepare by reading everything. Decide beforehand whom you want to meet and what benefits you would like to receive. Carry and hand out plenty of cards and literature about you and your business.

Continue to learn, grow and strive for success. Focus on building relationships and being rich in the resources of people. Also strive to fill the needs of others because, in time, you will reap the benefits. The benefits may not be the benefits you expect; they may be better and more satisfying. Make sure you're having fun.

10. Find common denominators. Common denominators are the thread that connects network partners. Without common interests, objective or and values, bonds cannot be created. And without bonds, solid and meaningful networks cannot be built.

Connect in your mind anything that your contacts may have in common and then build upon those similarities. Common interests, backgrounds and experiences make ideal ice breakers and pave the way to building deeper, more lasting relationships.

11. Bring value. Always have ideas, suggestions and insights to share. Help the other person out first; don't wait for them to give you a lead or connection.

Be prepared to happily give without return. Be prepared to happily give more than your share, more than is expected. Gain a reputation for generously giving value and you will never be alone or unappreciated.

12. Be honest, courteous and fair. Deliver what you promise and when you can, deliver more. Don't exaggerate or claim to be what you're not. Deliver on time, call on time and show up on time. Become known for your reliability and dependability. Show others that they can always count on you.

Treat everyone fairly and build a good reputation. Always be fair and ethical, it will gain you respect, admiration and tons of repeat business. Treat everyone with courtesy and respect and you will be treated with courtesy and respect in return. Build a great reputation. A terrific reputation is a commodity that endures, but that can be lost by just one lapse.

13. Follow up. After you first meet, keep in touch in a creative way. Send special notes or postcards, ones that have significance to topics you discussed. Write information about your contact's interests on the back of their business card. Then send them articles or information related to their interests.

Be quick to express your gratitude. Thank people for helping you and let them know how much you appreciate their aid with handwritten thank-you notes, emails, phone calls or gifts. Distinguish yourself by promptly expressing your thanks.

14. Keep referrers informed. As you build relationships, keep your network referrers in the loop. Let them know when you set up a meeting and fill them in on your progress. If you land a project, call them at once. And at each new step, express your thanks.

Remember that those who have helped you have a stake in the outcome of introductions or connections they made on your behalf. By keeping them informed, you will be keeping them on your team and keeping them involved, where you can draw on their help and support.

15. Look at the big picture. Try to see past the momentary, day-by-day activities that occupy your life and build toward your overall, life-time objectives. Sometimes taking nothing or less today will position you to gain far more tomorrow. Often, sacrificing today, will provide you with future benefits that will be far more meaningful. Enlarge your perspective so to see beyond the immediate and constantly reexamine your long-term goals.

CHAPTER 13

SURVEY SAYS— NETWORKING DON'T'S

"It's not who you know, it's who knows you!"
—Jill Lublin

In our research for this book, we asked a wide range of experienced networkers what they thought were the most important things to avoid when networking. The top, most frequently expressed responses are listed below. Please note that the list below does not place the responses we received the order that the respondents considered most important.

1. <u>Don't act desperate</u>. People prefer to associate with successful people. If they feel you're desperate they will avoid you like the plague. Most people will deal with desperate people when the have to, but when the job is done, they will run from them. So clearly communicate to your contacts that you're interested, but don't make them feel that if you don't achieve your objective you will slit your wrists.

2. <u>Don't sell</u>. Never enter into any networking situation with the intention of selling. Networking is not sales, its building relationships. If you try to sell, you may foreclose the possibility of forging an importance alliance. Be patient and don't try to land a contract at the first opportunity. If you sell to early or to hard, you will scare your contacts away. Instead, concentrate on building the relationship.

3. Don't monopolize. Respect the value and short supply of peoples' time. When you attend networking events and or have networking opportunities, appreciate that your contacts and those you meet are also attending to meet people and build relationships. Learn to separate business and social occasions and act appropriately at each. A business networking event is primarily a time for business. Sure you can socialize lightly, but if you're lonely or want to hang out with friends, attend social, not business, events.

4. Don't ask too soon. Avoid asking for help until you've developed a relationship with your contact. Most people will be put off, feel exploited and label you as a user when you come on too quickly or strongly. Be patient. Set the stage by expressing a sincere interest in others and getting to know them. Then when the relationship has formed, it may be time to ask.

5. Don't solicit competitors. Don't ask for or expect help from those who are in direct competition with you. Be realistic and don't ask others to do what you wouldn't like to do for them. Some competitors will be friendly, even generous, but don't push them. The help you request could cost them business, so why should they help you.

HARVEY MACKAY'S 10 BIGGEST NETWORING MISTAKES

1. Don't assume the credentials are the power. Every outfit is different. No organizational chart can tell you who the real decision maker is. You need a network to find out where the power is.

2. Don't confuse visibility with credibility. Don't join any organization to advance your own interest. Your motives will be as painfully obvious as a deathbed conversion.

3. Don't be a scnorrer. That's Yiddish for people who constantly take a little bit more than they're entitled to. Save your big favor requests for the big issues.

4. Don't say no for the other guy. Don't presume that someone within reach of your network would automatically say no.

5. Dance with the one that brung you. When someone in your network comes through, don't be a stiff. Dinner, flowers, a box of candy, or even just a phone call is a must.

6. Don't mistake the company's network for your network. If you're going to keep your job, your network has to be as good or better than your own company's network.

7. Don't be slow to answer the call. Don't stall. Even if you never expect to have your effort repaid. Remember that your network will be as fast broadcasting your failures as it is in broadcasting your successes.

8. It probably isn't just your network that's aging; its you. Make a genuine effort to modernize your skills and knowledge. Catch the zeitgeist.

9. Don't underestimate the value of the personal touch. Small businesses must know how to network with their customers and prospects by emphasizing a level of personal service and attention that the big businesses can't.

10. If you don't know, ask. Even if you do know, ask. To compete, draft a questionnaire and put it where your customers can pick it up.

6. Don't show off or brag. In most cases, show offs and braggarts only impress themselves. Nobody likes braggarts and blowhards, except their mothers, and that isn't always so. Usually, braggarts and blowhards are only in it for themselves, which is the antithesis of the philosophy of giving that underlies networking. People may tolerate boasters for a while, but not for long. Successful people usually have a choice of who to deal with and like most of us, steer clear of those we consider to be unpleasant, obnoxious or too self absorbed.

7. Don't interrupt. It's rude and turns everyone off. It tells people that you think that what you have to say is more important than what they are saying, which isn't a smart way to build relationships. Be patient and wait your turn. Most people notice and appreciate forbearance and courtesy. It builds respect, which is a great way to launch relationships.

8. Don't just talk about you. Besides being tedious, you won't learn anything by talking only about yourself. Plus, it irritates people. Talking only about you will make others feel that you've got such a strong involvement in yourself that you have no room for a relationship with them. Talk about yourself only when another person asks you about yourself, but make it brief. Then bring the conversation back to them. Hold your tongue or you could end up talking to yourself.

9. Don't play it by ear. Anticipate and be prepared. Try to determine beforehand the possibilities that could present themselves and be prepared. Think about the people you're likely to meet, what they may say and the situations you could encounter. Have a killer sound bite ready to deliver along with follow up information that they might request. Bring plenty of business cards, brochures and writing materials.

10. Don't misrepresent yourself. The purpose of networking is to build long-lasting, mutually beneficial relationships. If you pretend to be what you're not, sooner or later you will be caught and no one will associate with you. When you pretend to be what you're not, eventually you won't be able to deliver. If you can't deliver what you promise, the relationships you build won't be reciprocal and they certainly won't be long lasting.

11. Don't promise what you can't deliver. See above.

12. Don't pry. Be clear about what information you need, but don't ask questions about areas that seem confidential. Don't force someone to tell you, "Mind your own business." Begin by asking broad questions and the narrow the focus until the first sign of reluctance. When you sense hesitation or reluctance, immediately back off, let them off the hook. Don't go where you're not wanted or you will find yourself alone.

13. Don't linger with losers and "hanger-ons." Your time is valuable and if you let them, some people will take as much of it as you allow. They latch onto you, try to take whatever they can get that could help them and are hard to shake. Usually, they bring nothing to the table and want so much. Furthermore, they block the path for others to approach you. Some are so insistent and persistent that they force you to be harsh and blunt. They can make you feel guilty. Learn to recognize these leeches and cut them off before they completely drain you. Be polite, be courteous, but be firm or otherwise they simply won't let go.

14. <u>Don't overextend</u>. Select a few prime targets that you think you can realistically reach and put them on your A List. Don't shoot for everyone and everything. If you arrange to have breakfast or lunch with everyone you meet your weight will explode and your business will implode. Understand that there are limits to who to court and what you can achieve. Be realistic, concentrate your utmost efforts of a few worthy targets and place the rest on your B and C Lists. Keep in touch with your B List contacts by phone or e-mail.

15. <u>Don't be discouraged</u>. Most good things take time, patience and work. When you try to build relationships, you are attempting to become a part of someone's life and many desirable people won't let you right in. They want to know who you are, can you be trusted and do they want to spend time or be associated with you. Success usually takes trial and error and the errors can be difficult to take. Stick with it! Find network allies who can support you in these dire moments and hang in there until you succeed.

CHAPTER 14

SPECIAL TACTICS

"(1) Out of clutter find simplicity,
(2) From discord find harmony,
(3) In the middle of difficulty lies opportunity."
—Albert Einstein's
Three Rules Of Work

This chapter will cover:
- ❑ *Recommend meeting list*
- ❑ *Remembering names*
- ❑ *Adoption*
- ❑ *CEO Space's SNAP*
- ❑ *Accelerated dating*

In the course of writing this book, we came across a number of fascinating tactics that were primarily designed facilitate and/or speed up the networking process. Most of these methods focused on achieving quick end results, not gradually developing close network relationships. Some tactics were inventive adaptations of standard networking practices that their advocates swear by and claim will produce outstanding in results in short time spans.

In this chapter, we are including five special tactics that we consider most intriguing and adaptable. We know that all of these approaches won't work for everyone or in every situation. However, we hope that they or elements of them will inspire you and spark imaginative ways for you to create personally-tailored versions that will help you obtain the results you need.

As you read the following special tactics, use your imagination, be creative and have fun. Picture how they or parts of them could best serve you. Even consider mixing and matching elements from each of the following approaches until you find a hybrid that works for you.

Recommended meeting lists

Author Leonard Koren was invited to an event celebrating publication of a new book. When he arrived, he was handed a nametag and a card. His name was written on the card as was the statement, "People you should meet." Below that statement were the names of six individuals who the hosts though would interest Koren. In the course of the evening, Koren met several of those on his list and did indeed find most of them interesting.

Although Koren met equally interesting people who were not on his list, the fact that each person was given a list took on a life of its own, it became a topic of conversation. People talked about it all evening. Upon seeing others, they would check out his/her nametag and say, "Well, you're not on my list, but ____" or "Oh, you're on my list," and enter into conversations.

If you're hosting a networking event, recommending meeting lists can be both helpful and fun. Basically, it's a larger version of planning the seating arrangement for a dinner. In both cases, your goal is to connect people on the basis of how you think they will relate, which is fun—especially when they hit it off. In addition, the novelty of recommending meeting lists can serve as a great conversation starter.

Preparing recommended meetings lists can be long, arduous work and requires great networking skills. Like any mix-and-match process, many connections will immediately seem obvious while some mavericks will seem hopeless and test you matchmaking skills. However, often these strays connect with kindred spirits and the most unlikely combinations form the strongest relationships.

Recommended meeting lists force you to examine your guest roster, obtain knowledge about each guest and find common denominators that could lead to good connections. If you're hosting large events, it means lots of work. However, most guests will appreciate the time and effort you expended even if they hate the matches you recommended.

Remembering names

During our research for this book, people repeatedly explained that they were not good networkers because they couldn't remember the names of people they met. Successful networkers also revealed that they constantly struggle to remember names. Since most of them had some loose memory system, most of which didn't always work, so we turned to an expert.

Public speaker and marketing consultant Ken Glickman suffered from a faulty memory for names so he created a system that has trained him to remember well over 100 first names. Glickman concentrates on first names, which he feels is sufficient for networking meetings and events. However, he is clear that his system is a short-term approach. So don't expect it to work when you come across someone out-of-context who you met briefly at a conference last year.

According to Glickman, "Most people don't remember names because they don't really listen in the first place. However, they do remember people they like and admire because they pay attention to them."

"Everyone's favorite word is their own name. So if you want to make others feel important and good about themselves, call them by name." Glickman explains. "You can't make them feel special if you don't remember their name. And if you pretend that you know someone's name, you're usually going to get caught and no longer seen credible. People infer that if you're lying about that, what else are you untruthful about?"

To address his inability to remember names, Glickman developed a three-step technique that forced him to concentrate and listen. By mastering Glickman's system, you can teach yourself to remember those you meet. You can also avoid embarrassing moments when you can't recall the name of someone you just met. Improving your memory for names should help you network better and more confidently.

When Glickman meets someone new, he:

- Deliberately shakes his/her hand and repeats his/her first name several times during their initial conversation. For example, he might say, "Joe, it's nice to meet you. Where are your from Joe? And how long will you be here Joe?" Or, he will introduce Joe to someone else and say, "Joe this is Harry. Harry, Joe is here for the meeting."
- As soon as he/she walks away, but within 10 to 15 seconds, Glickman visualizes the person's face in his mind and repeats his/her name.
- About 30 seconds later, Glickman looks around the room for that person and when he spots him/her, has says his/her name.

Glickman's process requires you to listen, focus and connect the names and faces in your mind. The more you do it, the better you get.

When Glickman forgets peoples' names, he goes right up to them and states, "I've been having trouble remembering names," and he asks them their names. Glickman believes that when you admit not knowing their names, you can create a mental block and the quickest way to clear that block is to immediately ask.

Similarly, when you meet someone and can't remember his/her name, don't bluff or pretend. Promptly say, "I remember your face and I enjoyed our conversation so much last time, but I'm sorry I'm having trouble with names and I can't remember your name." Provide whatever context you can to show that you only forgot their name, not them. Then when they tell you their name, repeat it during the remainder of your conversation.

Adoption

Networking plays a vital role in at least half of the open adoptions in the United States, according to Renee Wall Rongen, the former Principal of the Adoption Resource Group. In an open adoption, couples that wish to adopt go through an agency, an attorney or find a birth mother who will agree to let them adopt her child.

Rongen advise couples on open adoptions of children born in the US. She encourages couples to design business cards that contain their:

- First names. The cards can also include last name if they wish
- Home address
- Email address
- Telephone number. Rongen suggests that couples install a separate number exclusively for adoption calls
- Photographs, especially if they are photogenic and
- A statement such as, "Loving couple looking to expand family through adoption," "Loving, financially-secure couple looking to form their family through adoption," or "Well-educated couple looking to adopt."

Rongen recommends three or four color cards printed on a glossy paper stock so photographs can be in color and the cards will stand out. Cards may also include bullet points for items that the couple wishes to stress such as their great health, existing family, financial security, education and others.

When their cards have been printed, Rongen advises her clients to compose a letter to everyone on their Christmas list and to all their business contacts.

In each letter that they send, the couples should enclose at least five of their cards.

The letter should state, "Dear _____, I feel awkward sending you this note, but we are trying to adopt a child and need your help. Today, adoption entails taping into our friends to ask if they know, or have heard, of someone— perhaps a friend, a neighbor or a relative—who is having a baby that she may want to place for adoption. If you do, please give her one of the cards we have enclosed and ask if we can call her.

Could you also post the enclosed cards at locations that birth mothers, birth fathers or their parents frequent. For example, obstetricians' offices, maternity shops, college campus bulletin boards, coffee shops, book stores, gyms, fitness centers and car washes."

Since some recipients, especially older and more traditional folks, might resent or be offended by such letters, Rongen suggests inclusion of a "get-out quick clause." Such clauses are also ideal for "spiritually grounded" people.

The clause should be placed at the bottom of the letter and should read, "If our request makes you uncomfortable, we ask you to please pray for us during this process."

NETWORKING NUGGET

Rongen instructs her clients to always carry plenty of their cards. A couple she was working with was attending a food festival where they met lots of new people. One couple asked Rongen's clients if they had any kids and they replied,

"No, but we're looking to adopt."

"Oh, wow, you should hook up with my neighbor's daughter," their new contact said.

So Rongen's clients handed the couple their card and asked them to give it to their neighbor's daughter. A week later, the girl called and they ended up adopting her child.

In addition, Rongen suggests that her clients network through the Internet by checking the numerous adoption sites and discussion groups. Many adoption sites allow couples to post a "Birth-Parent Letter," which contains their photographs and explains who they are, why they want to adopt and additional information. Rongen warns her clients to carefully screen all birth mothers who contact them through the Internet.

Finally, Rongen recommends that her clients send a separate, more formal letter, with their cards, to professionals such as attorneys, accountants, doctors and professors. She also advises them send similar letters to college spiritual centers and to college medical clinics, which is the first place many pregnant college girls turn. In this letter, Rongen's clients introduce themselves, state that they are hoping to adopt, explain why and explain what they can provide. The letters should also include the couple's photographs and ask the recipients to post their cards.

CEO Space's SNAP

CEO Space has developed a trademarked accelerated networking process that it calls SNAP. Here's how SNAP works.

At networking a meeting with 50 or more people, instead of networking by swapping business cards, five or six chairs are placed in a circle. There are no tables, only chairs. On the floor, in the center of each circle, are three items: (1) a large, brightly colored hat, (2) a glossy wand with a ball at one end and (3) a stack of "See Me" cards, which we will describe below.

The participants in each circle are seated in the chairs facing each other with their knees a few inches from the neighbor next to them. The circles where participants initially sit are their home circles. One member of each circle is designated to go first and he/she puts on the hat.

The SNAP session begins, when the designated member tells the other circle members, "Here's what I'm doing" and "Here's what I need next." Their messages should take no longer than 10 to 15 seconds and other members of the circles may ask questions that the speaker might use to sharpen his/her pitch. Speakers may use props such as photographs or illustrations of their work, copies of books they have written and samples of their products. They can also distribute cards or literature.

The key in delivering the message is to get right to the heart of the matter, clearly explain precisely what you need and not give extraneous information. When addressing circle members, participants should smile and connect with everyone in the circle, but move fast.

When the first speaker finishes delivering his/her message, the person seated to his/her left informs the other circle members what he/she is doing and what he/she needs. In turn, each circle member addresses the group until they go around the circle. The full round for all circle members to deliver their pitches takes only three minutes. The initial phase can be repeated twice to help all of the participants refine their messages.

After each circle member has delivered his/her pitch, the other members of the circle hand him/her a "See Me" card. The words "See Me" are printed across the top of the card followed by spaces where each participant writes his/her name, room number and email address. Seasoned CEO Space participants and those in CEO Space's week-long sessions, often have preprinted stickers with their contact information and their picture.

Below the contact information, the words "Yes! See Me! I am Your:" are printed in bold, upper-case letters. Below that line are three entries, which state:

A. Solution for _____

B. Introduction to a contact that will resolve your project (because I CAN influence them) _____

C. Introduction to a contact that "Can" resolve your project (they CAN do it!—I'll introduce you today) _____

- Item A tells the recipient, "I am the solution for your problem. I personally can provide what you need."
- Item B means that the giving party has a contact who can provide the solution the recipient needs and that the giving party has influence over his/her contact's decisions.
- Item C states that the giving party has a contact who can solve the recipient's problem, but the giving party does not influence his/her contact's decisions. It also conveys that the giving party will introduce the recipient to his/her contact today.

In the spaces provided after Items A, B and C, the giving party can write additional information. Or they can merely circle the letter on the card that indicates the level of help they can provide.

After giving See Me cards, the giving parties should make notes to themselves stating who they gave a card, the degree of help they indicated that they would provide and why. Therefore, when the recipient contacts them, they can remember why and how they though they could help. CEO Space encourages participants to give freely and promotes giving back. So those who provide high quality contacts, can receive substantial returns including fees, stock or both.

After the members go completely around their circle, the designated member, who is wearing the hat, stands up and runs around to the other circles. He/she jumps into seats vacated by other hat wearers, who have now moved to other circles. Hat wearers deliver their messages quickly and the circle members circle then give the hat wearer See Me cards listing the type of help they can provide. After receiving cards, or receiving no cards, the hat wearers move on to circles that they have not visited. The object is for the hat wearer to sit in at as many different circles as possible.

As the hat wearers run from circle to circle, some circles have a vacant seat. So members of those circles will wave the wands and call to hat wearers to inform them of the vacancy.

After a set time, usually three to five minutes, the hat wearer returns to his/her home circle and the hat is passed to the persons seated to his/her left. When a signal is given, the new hat wearer starts racing around to give his/her pitch to other circles. The process continues until each member of the circle has worn the hat and delivered his/her message at other circles. This is super networking; the practice of going beyond your own network.

"Super networking is the master skill of the new century. It is the process by which you invite and capture the contacts of your expanding network," CEO Space cofounder Bernhard Dohrmann explained. "Your network is not used for who they are, but for who they know. In this process, you rapidly develop connections and contacts for your purpose or agenda of the moment, which is to solve priorities one at a time, not five at a time. You use your network to resolve the priority of the moment primarily by who they know, which means you're super networking. If you solve them by who they are, you're only networking. Those who know a little bit about networking skills will always be outperformed by those who know how to super network."

CEO Space teaches that who you know in your own circle doesn't matter, even though you may have some great cards and great contacts. What does matter is connecting with as many circles you can and tapping into their resources.

After participants receive See Me cards, they must follow up. At SNAP sessions, people move so fast that they often need reminders to inform them why they offered help. The best approach is to contact them immediately after the SNAP session, show them their See Me card and set a firm time for further contact.

At SNAP sessions, CEO Space prefers as wide a mix as possible because diverse backgrounds produce more contacts. Similarly, "SNAP works better with larger groups because you have more resources for connectivity," according to Dohrmann.

"Most people ask for something that they want in the future. SNAP enables them to get what they need now," Author Barry Spilchuk, an experienced SNAP session leader explained.

When CEO Space holds sessions for corporate clients, it asks them to bring their key subcontractors, suppliers and vendors because they have insightful, creative solutions that companies can utilize. CEO Space believes that the presence of these resources help corporations unbottleneck roadblocks and develop customers. It also requests companies to bring their customers to SNAP sessions because customers will tell them how to get and satisfy more customers, if they'll only listen and let them.

Dohrmann believes that, "In a super networking session, you can accomplish more in 90 minutes than you ordinarily can in 90 days." He recommends that organizations hold SNAP sessions twice a year and require every participant to bring one new member or guest. If they do, Dohrmann is convinced that they will double club membership.

Accelerated dating

Networking has always been an integral part of dating. How many millions of people met their sweethearts through being "fixed up" on blind dates? Introductions, referrals and matchmaking are natural and time-honored practices for bringing single people together. Books, plays, movies and music celebrate them. And in this age when both women and men are swamped by busy, unrelenting, fast-tracked careers, dating has become a major industry.

Dating services are now a part of the landscape, they are everywhere, they proliferate. They come in every size, shape and form. They're in every city and all over the Internet. Virtually all of these services utilize some form of networking, connecting people in order to create meaningful relationships. One of the most interesting approaches is fast dating.

Accelerated dating, which is also known by other similar names including speed, fast, quick or express dating, is a matchmaking technique that was developed to facilitate rapid connections between single people and members of the opposite sex. In one evening, a single can meet and hold a number of uninterrupted conversations people who are looking to enter into in romantic relationships. In many ways, these conversations are nothing more than interviews to see whether the other is worthy of another shot.

Although multiple variations of fast dating exist, the following generally outlines how the process works.

A group of unmarried women and men gather at a restaurant, recreation center or other meeting room to meet and talk with one another. The group can have certain common denominators such as religion, ethnic background, interests, backgrounds and careers. Each group consists of an equal number of men and women. However, since more females tend to sign up, they may have to wait for a several sessions before there is an opening for them to participate. Those who attend pay an admission charge and the size of each group can vary.

The rooms where participants meet are usually set up with numbered tables. In most cases, the tables seat two, but occasionally they seat four. Each woman is assigned to a table for the evening. Each participant is given a form listing the names of the participants and a place to indicate whether he/she would like to see that person again.

The proceedings start when, at a given signal, each of the men goes to a separate table to conduct a one-on-one conversation with the woman assigned to that table for the evening. The host organizations usually suggest that the participants keep conversations light and avoid probing deeply into relationships or personal matters. Instead, they are encouraged to discuss their interests, families and where they live. Work and career can also be discussed broadly. Typical questions included what do you like to read, what movies do you like and what do you do weekends? Some host organizations provide suggested topics to help break the ice? During conversations, the level of intensity is deep.

After a set time, which can vary from three to fifteen minutes, a signal sounds. The signal directs the men to move to the next table where another woman is waiting. Depending on the size of the group, it can take two to three hours to go through the room and meet all of the men or women.

After each visit, both parties indicate on the form whether they would like to see that person again. At the end of the evening, the forms are collected by the host organization and correlated. If a man and woman both indicate on the form that they would like to see each other again, the host organization informs them both and gives them the other party's telephone number. The host organization usually provides this information within two or three days.

★☆★ Action steps ★☆★

---

1. Provide three examples of how you could adapt the concept of recommended meeting lists to enhance your networking efforts.

_____

_____

_____

2. Identify four places or events where you could practice remembering names.

_____

_____

_____

3. List three ways that you could accelerate your networking.

_____

_____

_____

4. Create up with three inventive ways to facilitate networking.

_____

_____

_____

CHAPTER 15

SUMMING UP

"Concentrate all your thoughts upon the work at hand.
The sun's rays do not burn until brought to a focus."
—Alexander Graham Bell

Now that you've completed this book, we want to thank you for reading it and for thinking about the information that we've provided. We know that we have covered a lot ground, so before we sign off, we would like to summarize and briefly reiterate some of the major points that go to the heart of networking. So pardon the repetition, but we are convinced these points are so essential that they can't be stressed too often.

Reading a book is one thing, but putting it's content in practice is completely different. Frequently, readers run into trouble because they don't know where to start or they try to implement all the information they've learned at once. When they try to take on too much, they usually get overwhelmed, become discouraged and don't continue further.

Give yourself a break. Take two or three days to let the information in this book to settle and percolate in your mind. Let your brain digest and clarify it. After a couple of days, concentrate on the book and see which of the areas we covered pop into your mind. Write down which topics come to mind, pick no more than three or four, review our discussions of them and start to master them.

Think about the advice Kim Yancy, Founder and Chief Marketing Officer and President of eWomenNetwork offers: "I think that you can never lose if you go to give, if you network to give. You just are not making—when you take the pressure off of yourself to engage with another person and your intention is I want to close this new deal, I want to get this contract, I want to get them to buy my product, you know what, that creates all the wrong energy for you. I think you can switch that entire gear and that entire feeling by moving yourself into that relationship and knowing that you are there to serve or to give and to be helpful as opposed to let me get my needs met first. Just slow down."

Follow the suggestions we made in this book and add ideas and approaches of your own. First, think all approaches through carefully and then practice implementing them with your family and close friends. For example, start by trying to identify the members of your existing network and how they can help. Train yourself to look everyone you know or meet in terms of how they could fit into your network. When that become routine, move on and try to implement other suggestions we offered.

Develop you own style. Try different approaches until you discover what feels comfortable. Move at your own pace and pay careful attention to how others respond. Monitor whether you're having fun and being successful. When you find approaches that that seem to work, practice them until they become natural and you no longer have to think about them. Move slowly, step by step and before you know it, you will be a master networker.

While you're practicing, remember:

1. Networking is the process of building and maintaining relationships, supportive alliances that help you and your network partners reach your goals. Good will and a good reputation create the foundation for a solid network. To successfully network you must constantly create good will and then build upon that good will to forge bonds that develop into close, meaningful relationships. In networking, building relationships should always be the networker's primary objective, building solid relationships is more important than short-term goals.

Every networking effort you make should be directed a building close and enduring relationships.

2. To create a diverse network. Construct a multi-faceted network filled with contacts who possess a wide variety of differing supportive skills, interests and backgrounds. Enlist partners who are expert in areas that differ from and compliment your expertise. The object of networking is to cover all of the bases and challenges you might face. Concentrate on recruiting network partners who fill in your gaps and shortcomings. Think of them as experts who are fluent in languages that you don't speak. Encourage them to teach you and expose you to areas that will broaden your knowledge and interests. If you're weak at marketing, turn to marketing experts. Don't enlist only people who duplicate your strengths because it will redundant and limit your growth and development.

3. Networking is based on giving generously and graciously. Although reciprocity is important, learn to give without expectation of return. Don't be deterred by the fact that people may not be as giving or as generous as you, just keep on giving. Always be willing to give and consciously look for opportunities to give. Initially, giving selflessly may difficult because of impatience or because you have immediate needs to fill, but keep giving. Unfortunately, the fruits of networking don't come overnight, in fact, they make take time, but if you stick with it, the magic will occur. The ideal time to build your network is when you are in a position to help others and you don't need their help in return. Help others whenever you can because it could motivate them to assist you when you need help.

4. To listen and observe. Let others carry the conversation and while they do, pay careful attention to what they say. If you let them speak, most people will disclose who they are, what they do and what they need. And, if after listening, you're still not sure, ask them directly. Show your interest by being attentive and ask probing questions. When you're attentive, others will be flattered. Never interrupt or break into a conversation. Wait, be patient and listen, your turn will come. Others will notice and appreciate your

forbearance. When the conversation turns to you, speak briefly and then move the conversation back to others and continue to listen. Listening and observing are the best ways to learn about others and develop strong connections.

5. That trust is an absolute prerequisite for building successful networks. Integrity counts; it provides a level of consistency that people can rely upon. The network partners you want to be affiliated with will not recommend or extend themselves for those who do not consistently deliver the best. Anything less will tarnish their reputations and limit their potential returns. Each and every member of your network must be completely confident that they can always rely upon you to provide expertise, excellent service, honesty, high standards, knowledge of their needs and the ability to make great matches. Don't promise if you can't deliver, don't exaggerate or misrepresent.

6. To spot lead for your partners. Establish your value to your network by developing the ability to spot viable leads and opportunities for your network members and recommend good matches. To recognize opportunities, requires you to know about and understand the needs of both your contacts and your network partners. When you demonstrate that you consistently look for and identify opportunities for your network partners, you will become a valuable resource upon which they will increasingly rely. If you can also match your network partners with others who can provide them with what they need, your value will soar.

7. That networks are built around the exchange of information and nourished by a constant stream of information. To efficiently utilize this information requires expert knowledge (1) to recognize the full implications of the data received and what it means and (2) about the members of your network, their capabilities, capacities and needs. To build and maintain a successful network requires expertise. Your expertise is the exchange that you give to your network partners in return for their help The more knowledgeable you become, the more valuable you will be to potential network partners. By becoming an expert, you will make yourself more attractive to those who can give

you the greatest help. People with influence want to associate with the best and surest route to top is by becoming an expert.

8. To know your purpose. Before selecting networking targets, clarify in your mind exactly what you want. If you fail to precisely request what you seek you risk getting less than you desire and can create misunderstandings. Develop a compelling vision that you can see and feel. Actually picture yourself at the point when you have achieved your objective. Before you begin to network identify realistic targets and research them thoroughly. In forming alliances, ask if your targets are individuals who you want to do business with, hang out with and/or be associated with? Select your targets precisely and limit the number you pursue. Often, when you try to corral too many, you end up landing few, if any. Don't shoot for the biggest stars unless you are convinced that you have a realistic chance and solid plan for reaching them. Identify all possible roadblocks that could block or delay your success.

9. To build a terrific networking toolkit. Develop a compelling sound bite that you can reel off in 10 to 15 seconds to explain who you are, what you do and how you can help. Make it a grabber that immediately captures your audience's attention. Before writing your sound bite, be sure that you clearly know what it is that you do. Ask your customers or clients, even if you think you know. Practice delivering your sound bite until you can clearly and confidently deliver it. If, after delivering your sound bite, listeners want additional information, give them your brochure, other print materials or a verbal description. Always carry a stack of your business cards and never leave home without your address list, calendar and writing materials, which are now easy to have on hand in PDAs and similar devices.

10. To follow up. Create a contact organization system that will keep your records current. Maintain a detailed database on your Rolodex, mobile device or address book, investigate the numerous computer programs that provide contact-organizing services or start a card file. Record as much information on your contacts as you can uncover including their business and personal backgrounds and interests. Enter new

contact information promptly and update your entire database at least every three months. When your network partners give you a lead or referral, keep them posted on your progress as it develops and always express your thanks in handwritten notes, email or telephone calls or by giving gifts.

ABOUT THE AUTHOR

RICK FRISHMAN, publisher at Morgan James Publishing in New York and founder of Planned Television Arts (now called Media Connect), has been one of the leading book publicists in America for over 35 years. Rick works with many of the top book editors, literary agents, and publishers in America, including Simon and Schuster, Random House, Wiley, Harper Collins, Pocket Books, Penguin Group and Hyperion Books. He has worked with bestselling authors such as Mitch Albom, Bill Moyers, Stephen King, Caroline Kennedy, Howard Stern, President Jimmy Carter, Mark Victor Hansen, Nelson DeMille, John Grisham, Hugh Downs, Henry Kissinger, Jack Canfield, Alan Deshowitz, Arnold Palmer, and Harvey Mackay.

Morgan James Publishing publishes fiction and nonfiction books and by authors with a platform who believe in giving back. Morgan James gives a portion of every book sold to Habitat for Humanity.

Rick has also appeared on hundreds of radio shows and more than a dozen TV shows nationwide, including Oprah and Bloomberg TV. He has also been featured in the *New York Times, Wall Street Journal, Associated Press, Selling Power Magazine, New York Post*, and scores of other publications.

He has appeared on stage with notables such as The Dalai Lama, Sir Richard Branson, T. Harv Eker, Jack Canfield, Mark Victor Hansen, Tony Hsieh, David Bach, Brian Tracy, and Brendon Burchard.

Rick is the coauthor of thirteen books, including national bestsellers *Guerrilla Publicity, Networking Magic, Where's Your Wow* and *Guerrilla Marketing for Writers*. His thirteenth book, *The 250 Rules of Business* with co-author Steven Schragis was published in July of 2013.

Rick has a BFA in acting and directing and a BS in communications from Ithaca College. He is a sought-after lecturer on publishing and public relations and a member of PRSA and the National Speakers Association.

Rick and his wife Robbi live in Long Island, New York with their two Havanese puppies, Cody and Cooper. They have three children: Adam, Rachel, and Stephanie.

Go to http://www.rickfrishman.com for more information and to get Rick's Million Dollar Rolodex.

ABOUT THE AUTHOR

JILL LUBLIIN

With 200+ speaking engagements each year, master publicity strategist and consultant, and bestselling author, Jill Lublin, consistently wows audiences worldwide with her entertaining and interactive keynotes, seminars, and training programs on publicity, networking, and influence marketing.

Jill has shared her powerful networking and publicity strategies on the stages of Tony Robbins, T. Harv Eker, Jack Canfield, Mark Victor Hansen, Loral Langemeier, Richard Simmons, and many others. Additionally, thousands of people have attended her popular "Crash Course in Publicity", which she teaches live several times a month at locations around the U.S. and Canada, as well as a live online webinar. Her popular home study system is used by clients worldwide who are ready to create greater success and revenues for themselves and their companies.

Over the past 25 years, Jill has worked with ABC, NBC, CBS, and other national and international media as a highly regarded publicity expert. She has been featured in *The New York Times, Women's Day, Fortune Small Business, Entrepreneur,* and *Inc.* magazines.

Jill is the author of three bestselling books, including: *Get Noticed... Get Referrals* (McGraw-Hill), *Networking Magic* (Morgan James), and *Guerilla*

Publicity (Adams Media), which is regarded as the "PR Bible". With three national bestselling books, Jill is acknowledged as the go-to person for building success through influence marketing, networking, and publicity. She is also the Producer and Host of the TV show, "Messages of Hope", which inspires people to take positive action to improve their lives and create a better world.

In addition to her speaking engagements, Jill trains and consults with executives, sales teams and marketing departments in Fortune 500 companies, as well as in small-to-medium-sized companies. Her innovative influence marketing and publicity techniques consistently increase bottom line results for her clients.

Visit www.PublicityCrashCourse.com/freegift or call 415-883-5455 for more information.

REFERENCE MATERIALS

RECOMMENDED READING LIST

Networking for People Who Hate Networking: A Field Guide for Introverts, the Overwhelmed, and the Underconnected—Devora Zack, Berrett-Koehler Publishers, 2010.

Networking Like a Pro: Turning Contacts into Connections—Ivan Misner, Entrepreneur Press, 2010

Networking Bible—Barrie Sosinsky, Wiley, 2009

How to Win Friends and Influence People—Dale Carnegie, Simon & Schuster, Reissued 2009

Never Eat Alone: And Other Secrets to Success, One Relationship at a Time—Keith Ferrazzi, Crown Press, 2005

Break Through Networking: Building Relationships that Las—Lillian D. Bjorseth, Duoforce Enterprises, 2003.

Capsules: Top 25 Tips & Creative Remedies for Women and Small Business Owners—Robyn Levin, Centerpiece Publishing (2003) eBook.

Crappy to Happy: Small Steps to Big Happiness Now—Get Clients Now!—C.J. Hayden, Amacom (1999).

Guerrilla Publicity: Hundreds of Sure Fire Tactics to Get Maximum Sales for Minimum Dollars—Jay Conrad Levinson, Rick Frishman and Jill Lublin, Adams Media Corp. (2002).

How To Work A Room: The Ultimate Guide to Savvy Socializing in Person and Online—Susan RoAne, Quill (2000).

I-Power: The Secrets of Great Business in Bad Times—Martin Edelston and Marion Buhagiar, The Greenwich Institute for American Education (1992).

Is Your Net Working: Complete Guide to Building Contacts and Career Visibility—Anne Boe and Bettie B. Youngs, John Wiley & Sons (1989).

Knock 'Em Dead 2004—Martin Yate, Adams Media Corp. (2002).

Learn to Power Think: A Practical Guide to Positive and Effective Decision Making—Caterina Rando, Chronicle Books (2002).

Make Your First Million in Network Marketing: Proven Techniques You Can Use to Achieve Financial Success—Mary Christensen and Wayne Christensen, Adams Media Corp. (2001).

Nonstop Networking: How to Improve Your Life, Luck, and Career—Andrea R. Nierenberg, Capital Books, Inc. (2002).

Power Networking Second Edition, 59 Secrets for Personal & Professional Success—Donna Fisher, Sandy Vilas and Marilyn Hermance, Bard Press (2000).

Secrets of Savvy Networking: How to Make the Best Connections for Business and Personal Success—Susan RoAne

Streetwise Business Tips: 200 Ways to Get Ahead in Business, Most of Which I Learned the Hard Way—Bob Adams, Adams Media Corp. (1998).

The Everything Start Your Own Business Book: From the Birth of Your Concept and Your First Deal, All You Need to Get Your Business Off the Ground—Richard Mintzer and Rich Mintzer, Adams Media Corp. (2002).

The Smart Woman's Guide to Networking—Joyce Hadley and Betsy Sheldon, Career Press (1995).

The Tipping Point: How Little Things Can Make a Big Difference—Malcolm Gladwell, Little Brown and Company (2000).

The 25 Sales Skills: They Don't Teach at Business School—Stephan Schiffman, Adams Media Corp. (2002).

21 Laws of Influence—Hellen Davis, Indaba Press (2003).

ORGANIZATION LISTINGS

AmSpirit Business Connections
P.O. Box 30724
Columbus, OH 43230
888-509-5323
www.amspirit.com

BNI International
199 S. Monte Vista, Suite 6
San, Dimas CA 91773
800-825-8286 (Outside
Southern California)
909-305-1811 (Fax)
909-305-1818 (Inside
Southern California)
www.bni.com

BPO Elks of the USA
2750 N. Lakeview Avenue
Chicago, IL 60614-1889
773-755-4700
773-755-4790 (Fax)
www.elks.org

Chamber of Commerce
(World Directory)
www.chamberofcommerce.com
Craigslist
www.craigslist.org

eWomenNetwork
14900 Landmark Boulevard
Suite 540
Dallas, TX, 75254
972-620-9995
www.eWomenNetwork.com

Executive Moms
www.executivemoms.com
First Tuesdays
www.firsttuesday.com

CEO Space International, Inc.
3030 Starkey Blvd.
Suite 270
Trinity, FL 34655

Kiwanis International
3636 Woodview Trace
Indianapolis, IN 46268-3196
317- 875-8755
317- 879-0204 (Fax)
www.kiwanis.org

Leads Club (Ali Lassen's)
PO Box 279
Carlsbad, CA 92018
800-783-3761
www.leadsclub.com

LeTip International, Inc.
P.O. Box 178130
San Diego, CA 92177-9926
800-25-LETIP (53847)
858-490-2744 (Fax)
www.letip.com

Lions Clubs International
300 W 22nd Street
Oak Brook IL 60523-8842
630-571-5466
www.lionsclubs.org

**National Association of
Female Executives**
260 Madison Avenue, 3rd Floor
New York, NY 10016
www.nafe.com
800-927-6233

**National Association of
Women Business Owners**
8405 Greensboro Drive, Suite 800
McLean, VA 22102
Telephone: (703) 506-3268
Fax: (703) 506-3266
www.nawbo.org/

Network Associates (NY)
147 Hazelwood Drive
Jericho, NY 11753
516-446-4144
516-937-5234 (Fax)
Skrauser@aol.com

Network Associates (Fla.)
19496 Island Ct. Dr.
Boca Raton, FL 33434
561-477-6626
561-477-5295 (Fax)
Skrauser@aol.com

Rotary International
1560 Sherman Avenue
Evanston, IL 60201
847-866-3000
847-328-8554 or 847-328-8281
(Fax)
www.rotary.org

Shared Vision Network
10300 W. Charleston Blvd
Ste 13-227
Las Vegas, NV 89135
702-284-5233
702-446-5565 (Fax)
www.sharedvisionnetwork.com

Soroptimist International
Two Penn Center Plaza
Suite 1000,
Philadelphia, PA 19102-1883
215-557-9300
215- 568-5200 (Fax)
www.soroptimist.org

CPSIA information can be obtained
at www.ICGtesting.com
Printed in the USA
BVHW031447100419
545158BV00004B/647/P

9 781614 487340